Lulu's Crochet Doll Family

8 adorable dolls and accessories to crochet

Sandra Muller

from the Lulu Compotine blog

SEARCH PRESS

The author

Lulu Compotine

@luciennecompotine

A graduate in fine arts, specializing in textiles, Sandra – the woman behind Lulu Compotine – loved handicrafts from an early age. Sewing, knitting, painting, drawing, crafts and modelling have always been a part of her daily activity. Around the age of eight, she began designing and making clothes for her dolls and creating a whole little world for them with accessories, tea sets, furniture and doll's houses.

She fell for the charms of crochet some ten years ago when making a cuddly toy for her daughter. She quickly became passionate about this new craft and has not put down her crochet hook since!

Over the intervening years, she has made innumerable little characters who populate her children's bedrooms and all the bookshelves. Instagram became the display window for her creations, which were received with enthusiasm. She then decided to make a career of it, setting up her Lulu Compotine business in 2018 and selling downloadable tutorials from her Etsy shop. These include a number of soft toys (mostly rabbits, her first love) and countless dolls to dress, along with some gorgeous accessories, all rooted in her childhood imagination.

Following the success of *Lulu's Crochet Dolls*, this second book gives you the opportunity to grow your collection of crochet friends and use your imagination to make this family your own.

Blog: www.lucompotine.com

Instagram: @luciennecompotine

Etsy shop: www.etsy.com/fr/shop/LuluCompotine

LA PRINCESSE AU PETIT POIS
Mausi geht schwimmen
Lars Klinting
NEUE BRIEFE VON FELIX
Briefe von Felix
de poche
Les poupées de Sosole crochet & tricot
Daria Vild
POUPÉES RÉTRO AU CROCHET
Laetitia Bleas
Poupée Pom'ette et sa garde-robe
Séverine Dingemans
Le monde merveilleux de KHUC CAY
Khuc Cay
KHUC CAY
KERRY LORD
Crochet Zodiac Dolls
Yan Schenkel
Khuc Cay
Khuc Cay
Vivyane Veka
Soledad IGLESIAS SILVA
Camille Lepecq
JULIA DUPÉ
HELLO Amigurumi
Happy Childhood Day

Introduction

This little family appeared in my imagination in the form of a story, the kind we used to tell each other as children in the playground, the stories that began, 'Let's pretend that...'. We would act out these stories in our bedrooms, alone with our dolls and then started inventing them all over again to tell our own children. You may have acted out stories with the dolls from my previous book: making them pretty outfits for each season, neatly arranged in little boxes; or building dolls' houses just for them. Maybe you took photographs of them and shared them on social media. Some people even impishly took them out of their bags when we met, with a knowing smile, as if we were sharing a secret. Perhaps it is the secret of rediscovered childhood.

All these beautiful memories have led me to imagine the little family in this book and to share it with you. I like to think that there is a child within all of us.

This is the story of a family getting ready to celebrate the youngest child's birthday. A story that begins with 'Let's pretend...'. I'll leave you to imagine the rest!

This is a story that has been brought to life a second time under the wonderful pencil strokes of Céline Bonnaud...

Lulu Compotine

Please note that UK crochet terms are used throughout this book.
For US equivalents please refer to the table on page 12.

My Guest

Céline Bonnaud

@les_loulous_de_guibo

Céline and I met via Instagram, each discovering what the other one made at almost the same time. What a wonderful chance encounter! It was as if, at first glance, all the crocheted dolls that I had in my head were reflected in a mirror. As if by some magic they were coming to life under her pencil. A revelation!

Since then we have met in person and enjoy a lovely creative partnership. So it seemed like an obvious step to both of us to pay a little homage to this friendship on the pages of our respective books.

I was so excited when Céline sent me the illustrations of my little family!

Find Céline on Instagram @les_loulous_de_guibo
and check out her online shop www.leslouloudeguibo.com

Thanks

First of all, a big thank you to **Viviane**, my editor, for believing in me the first time and then trusting me again with this book. A big thank you also to **Marine** for her enthusiasm and support throughout the creative process and to **Christine** for her wonderful layouts.

Thank you to **my whole family**, especially **my husband**, for supporting and encouraging me in this new project. Special regards for **my children**, who were my first source of inspiration and who have been my staunchest supporters in this new adventure.
I love you all.

Thank you to DMC France, once again a partner in this book, for their magnificent yarns in such beautiful colours, which were used to create all these characters.

Thank you to all **my wonderful testers** for their loyalty and kindness and especially to **Justine** and **Caroline** for their invaluable help.

Kind regards also to **Julia @cotonetgourmandises**, who followed everything from afar (geographically speaking) with such consideration and encouragement.
Thank you for being by my side.

Thank you from the bottom of my heart to my guest **Céline**, **@les_loulous_de_guibo**, who has made such gorgeous illustrations of my little family. We were so lucky to be publishing our books at the same time, which gave me a real creative boost. My little yarn family truly came to life through our discussions and her nimble fingers.

Thank you to **my dear friends** who have supported me on this journey and who always gave me good advice (I might not always follow it, but it definitely helps me to get out of a rut!).
I owe you so much. You're amazing!

And above all, thank you to **you, dear crocheters**, without whom this book would never have seen the light of day, for all your beautiful creations, your magnificent interpretations of Lulu's Dolls and the incredible welcome you gave to my first book. I love the scenes you post, your lovely shares, your kind words and your boundless encouragement, which gave me wings and inspired me to offer you this little crochet family. I hope you enjoy them and find them as inspiring as I did when they first appeared in my imagination. May this book bring you many happy hours of crocheting!

Sandra

Contents

Charlie
THE BOY TWIN

Penny
THE GIRL TWIN

Jean
THE GRANDPA

Lucie
THE GRANDMA

Materials

Basics

You will need these tools and materials for all the projects in this book, so make sure you have them close to hand:

- **1 round-ended darning (or tapestry) needle** for sewing the different parts of the work together;
- **1 small pair of pointed scissors**;
- **round-headed pins** for holding the pieces together during the making up process and to mark the location of things such as the eyes;
- **dark-coloured embroidery thread** (or even the cotton yarn used for crocheting the dolls) to embroider the eyes; or if you prefer you can use 6mm (¼in) safety eyes.
  If the doll is for a child of under the age of three, it is safer to embroider the eyes.
- **a stitch marker** so you can keep track of the rounds (I use a strand of yarn in a contrasting colour that I move as I go so I know where I've got to);
- **pipe cleaners (chenille sticks)** to slip into the dolls' necks to make their heads more stable. Pipe cleaners can be bought in tobacco shops and are used to clean smokers' pipes! You may be able to use a cotton bud (cotton swab) instead;
- **a little bit of red wax crayon** rubbed on to cloth; used to give your dolls' faces a rosy glow.

Yarns

The projects in this book have been crocheted using yarn by DMC, who make a great range of colours, but feel free to use equivalent yarns if you prefer, of the same type and thickness.

However, it is up to you to select the yarn that you want to use. If you opt for a different yarn, you must always ensure that you use a hook intended for one weight less than that given on the ball band.

- **DMC Natura Just Cotton** (4-ply/fingering) cotton yarn, 50g/1¾oz/155m/170yd, for all the dolls and accessories.
- **DMC Merino Essentiel 3** (4-ply/fingering) merino blend, 50g/1¾oz/200m/218yd for some of the clothes.

Both worked using a 2.25mm (UK 13, US B1) crochet hook.

- **Hobbii Diablo** (1–3-ply/lace weight) yarn, 40% acrylic, 30% mohair, 30% polyamide blend, 50g/1¾oz/225m/246yd, or **Hobbii Mohair Delight** (medium/worsted) 50% mohair, 50% acrylic blend, 50g/1¾oz/150m/164½yd, have also been used for the dolls' hair, worked with 3mm (UK 11, US C2/D3) and 3.5mm (UK 9, US E4) crochet hooks. I like the fuzzy look they give hair and certain other accessories. However, you can crochet them using the same yarn that you have used for the dolls themselves *(see instructions on page 17)*.

Yarn colours

For each project, you will find the yarn colours required to make them.
One ball of each main colour is enough to make two or three dolls (depending on their size).

DMC Natura Just Cotton:
(A) Acanthe (yellow) 81
(B) Azur (blue-green) 56
(C) Bamboo (lime green) 76
(D) Bourgogne (wine red) 34
(E) Cinnamon 37
(F) Coral 18
(G) Dragée (baby pink) 404
(H) Eider (blue) 878
(I) Gardenia (off-white) 36
(J) Géranium (rose pink) 52
(K) Gerbera (pink) 98
(L) Giroflée (mustard yellow) 85
(M) Glacier (pale blue) 87
(N) Green Valley (dark green) N14
(O) Grey 121
(P) Silver Grey 09
(Q) Ibiza (white) 01
(R) Ivory 02
(S) Lin (linen/taupe) 78
(T) Black 11
(U) Lobelia (dusty pink) 82
(V) Nacar (off-white) 35
(W) Sable (pale grey) 03
(X) Siena (brown) 41
(Y) Star Light (denim blue) N27
(Z) Sunflower (pale yellow) 16

(AA) Tropic Brown (dark brown) 22
(BB) Zaphire (black) N28

DMC Merino Essentiel 3:
(CC) Brick (orange-red) 953
(DD) Light Grey 962
(EE) Dark Taupe 959

Hobbii Diablo:
(FF) Caramel (brown) 15
(GG) Yellow Ochre 18
(HH) Honey (orange) 49
(II) Light Grey 04
(JJ) Natural White 02

Hobbii Mohair Delight:
(KK) Cinnamon 34

D·M·C
3/0 2.20mm Tulip

Hooks

I have made all the projects in this book using a **2.25mm (UK 13, US B1) crochet hook**. Feel free to adapt depending on how you crochet: if your stitches are loose, use a smaller hook (2mm, UK 14, US A0) and if they are very tight, go for a larger one (2.5mm, UK 13/12, US B1/C2) so the stuffing is not visible through the stitches.

The size of the crochet hook will also depend on the thickness of the yarn. Opt for a hook one size smaller than that given on the yarn band to make the stitches denser.

To crochet the yarn for the dolls' hair, I have used **3mm (UK 11, US C2/D3)** and **3.5mm (UK 9, US E4) crochet hooks**.

You may need to use a different size depending on your crocheting technique and the yarn you have chosen.

Note: the hook sizes used are specified at the start of the instructions for each project.

I use ergonomic hooks with a silicon or plastic handle as I find them more pleasurable to work with than a metal or bamboo hook. It is up to you to decide which one you prefer.

Stuffing

The projects may be stuffed with the **synthetic stuffing** widely used for cushions and soft toys (wash-resistant and treated to deter mites). Make sure you distribute it evenly and stuff the doll so it is firm but not pushing the stitches apart. I use **a wooden skewer** or **a crochet hook handle** to get the stuffing into narrow areas and push in a small amount at a time.

For the dolls, **it is important to make sure you have stuffed the neck and the base of the head properly to ensure it holds well**. For more stability I sometimes insert a pipe cleaner (chenille stick), approximately 8cm (3¼in) in length, between the neck and base of the head – this holds the head securely in place, especially with larger dolls that have heavier heads. I prepare the neck hole with a wooden skewer and then slide the pipe cleaner (chenille stick) into it. I then pad it out with a little more stuffing all round. The 'adult' dolls in this book have a cone-shaped tube section up the neck to make the head more stable. I slip a pipe cleaner into it.

For some of the dolls, you will also need a few small buttons, some cardboard or some wire, but this will be specified in the list of materials required for each project.

Abbreviations

The projects in this book are written using UK crochet terms. For US equivalents, please see below:

UK		US	
blo	back loop only		
ch	chain		
ch sp	chain space		
dc	double crochet	**sc**	single crochet
dc2tog	double crochet 2 stitches together	**sc2tog**	single crochet 2 stitches together
dec	decrease		
dtr	double treble	**tr**	treble crochet
flo	front loop only		
htr	half-treble crochet	**hdc**	half-double crochet
htr2tog	half-treble crochet 2 stitches together	**hdc2tog**	half-double crochet 2 stitches together
inc	increase		
MR	magic ring		
pc	popcorn stitch		
rep	repeat		
sk	skip	**miss**	
sl st	slip stitch		
st(s)	stitch(es)		
tr	treble crochet	**dc**	double crochet
yrh	yarn round hook	**yo/yoh**	yarn over/yarn over hook

Techniques

All the projects in this book are of an intermediate level, but if you are a beginner, don't hesitate to give them a go; you won't come across any major difficulties.

- **Start a project with a magic ring**

  (or a slip knot if it is easier for you.) *(See page 18.)*

- **Working in spiral rounds**

  The principle is to work in a circle, forming incomplete rounds, like a never-ending spiral. At the end of a round, crochet directly into the first stitch of the previous round without joining with a slip stitch.

***Note:** to keep track of how many stitches you have worked, place a stitch marker (a contrasting piece of yarn, for example) on the first stitch of the round and move it to the beginning of the next round as you go.*

- **Working in rows**

  Rows start with a foundation chain. Work the row into this chain then at the end of the row, turn it over and chain the given number of stitches before starting the new row.

- **Working round a foundation chain**

  Start by working the required number of chain stitches, then crochet along the top loops of the chain stitches from right to left; move around to the other side of the chain and crochet along the bottom loops of the chain stitches until you are back at the initial stitch. Join with a slip stitch in the first stitch (this last stage is only valid if you are working in the round, but not in spiral rounds).

- **Working round a foundation chain**

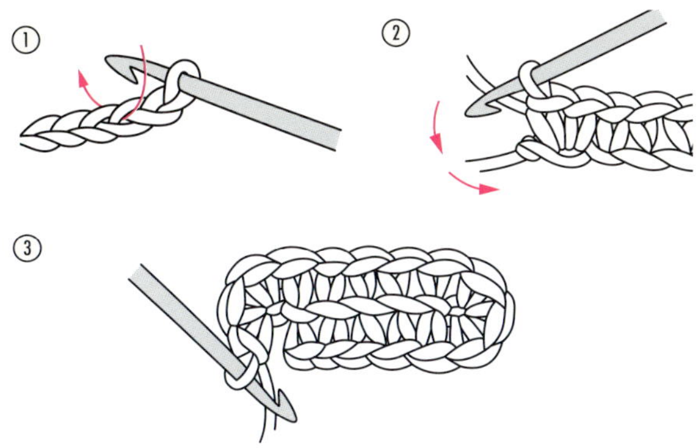

- **Fastening off**

  In this book, each time it says, 'fasten off', you need to work one chain stitch, cut the thread, then pull it through the chain to tie off. Make sure to leave a tail long enough to be able to weave it in, or even use it to sew a subsequent seam (this last point will be specified for each model).

- **Weaving in ends**

  For stuffed parts (such as the body), thread a darning needle with the tail of yarn and take it straight through the stuffed part. Bring it out at the other end. Cut off any excess yarn and using the point of the needle, push the end of the yarn back inside the stuffing to hide it. For other parts (such as clothes, etc.) weave the yarn through the stitches for a few centimetres or inches on the wrong side of the work, ensuring that it is not visible from the right side, then trim off any excess.

- **Changing yarn colour**

The simplest technique, which is also my preferred method, consists of changing colour on the last yarn round hook of the previous stitch, even if this results in a little join.

Work the first part of the double crochet (first yarn round hook) in the initial colour (there are two loops on the hook), then finish the stitch (second yarn round hook). using the new colour. This first stitch will still be in the initial colour, but the next will be in the new colour. Cut the initial yarn and knot to secure.

If you are working stripes, leave both yarns on the back of the work throughout, alternating them according to the instructions.

①

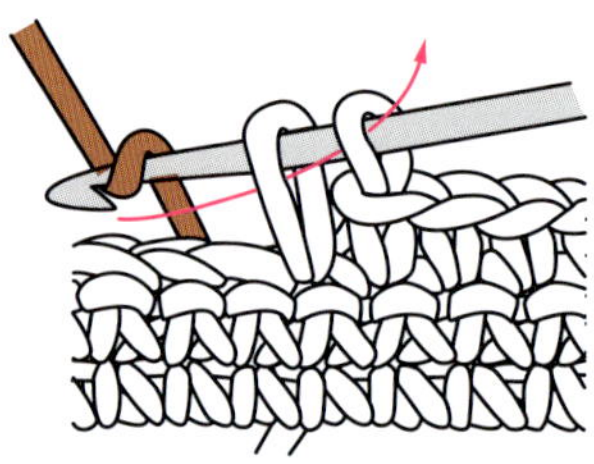

②

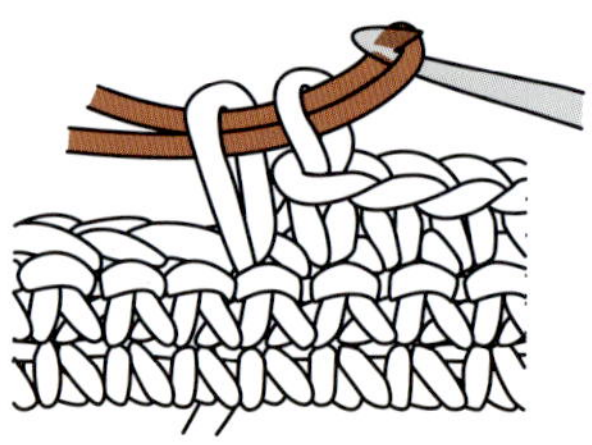

- **Joining yarn**

The easiest method is to tie a small flat knot with the end of the yarns that you want to join and position the knot so it cannot be seen on the right side of your work. When you have finished, weave in the ends of yarn on any pieces that are not stuffed (such as clothing).

- **Differentiating right side and wrong side**

On the right side of the work you can see that there are little Vs on each stitch.

On the wrong side, you can see little horizontal bars.

***Note:** to help orientate yourself, the starting yarn is always on the inside of the work. As the work gets taller (when you continue in rounds after the increases) there is often a tendency to start working on the wrong side, especially on smaller pieces such as legs or arms.*

- **Sewing up the arms by sewing the two sides together**

Start by pinching the upper edge to bring the two sides of the stitches of the last round together, then work one row of double crochet (or another stitch, depending on the instructions for each project), passing the hook through a stitch on each side at the same time.

- **Attaching the legs**

Starting from the second leg, crochet the specified number of chain stitches (this creates the gap between the legs), then crochet into all the top stitches of the first leg, work double crochets in each chain stitch of the gap between the legs, then work into the top stitches of the second leg.

- ## Sewing the pieces together (whipstitch)

Position the pieces to be sewn together as instructed (use pins to hold in place), then sew up using whipstitch.

To sew on the arms, for example, insert a darning needle under the two loops of the arm and do the same under the corresponding stitch of the body *(see photo 1)*. Pull the yarn tight *(see photo 2)*. To secure the seam, bring the yarns out through a stitch in the body, at the same place and tie them in a double knot *(see photos 3 and 4)*. Then pull them back inside the work to conceal.

Whipstitch

Position the two pieces right sides together. Insert a darning needle under the loop(s) of a stitch on the first piece and do the same in the corresponding stitch of the other piece. Repeat as many times as necessary, maintaining a regular tension to ensure an even seam.

- ## Creating a face

This is my favourite bit – the stage when the little character comes to life and starts to tell me stories. Personally, I prefer to embroider the eyes with a dark embroidery thread or a strand of cotton (of the same thickness as the yarn used to crochet the doll) rather than clipping on safety eyes, but it also depends on the project.

To embroider the eyes, I use straight stitch over a single stitch height, inserting the crochet hook in the two adjacent holes. I pass the yarn over twice to make them thicker. If you are using embroidery thread, you need to oversew three or four times. Before you begin, mark the position of the eyes with pins so you are sure it is correct.

You could also add some freckles *(see photo 5)* or some rosy cheeks *(see photo 6)*.

To add some colour to the cheeks, I rub a red wax crayon hard on a small piece of white cloth, then I rub that gently over the stitches in a circular motion. If you have added too much, rub again with a clean cloth.

- ### Adjusting the size of the clothing

The size of crocheted garments varies a lot depending on your personal crocheting style, especially if they are made with half-treble crochet stitches, which are often worked more loosely. Do not hesitate to change the size of your crochet hook if the garments seem too big to you (in which case use a smaller hook). It is well worth trying them on the doll as you are making them. You can also adapt the length of the skirts, dresses, trousers and sleeves by working an additional round or row, or one less.

- ### Tip for dressing your dolls

Always put clothes on in the following order: first the sweater, then the trousers and finally the shoes.

- ### Making spectacles

You need some wire, approximately 35cm (14in) in length and yarn in the colour of your choice *(see photos 7 and 8)*.

Start with the structure:

Identify the centre of the wire and wrap the first part around a little plastic lid or stopper (approximately 2.5cm/1in diameter) to form the first 'lens'. Fold the wire on each side of this lens to form one arm of the spectacles and the bridge of the nose *(see photo 9)*.

Leave around 1cm (½in) of wire for the bridge, then wrap the wire around the plastic cylinder again to create the second 'lens' *(see photo 10)*.

Then shape the second arm and cut the wire *(see photo 11)*. To hold the spectacles in place more securely, you can make a little loop at the ends of the arms. Use pliers to close up the spaces where the wires meet. For rectangular spectacles, use something like a plastic brick or an eraser to shape the lenses and round off the bottom to the shape you like (such as for Father's spectacles).

Then wind the cotton yarn round and round the structure, sticking into place with a glue stick and starting at the end of one of the arms. You need to make a tiny little ball of yarn so you can pass it through the hole of the 'lenses'. Cut the yarn and glue the end to secure in place. Wrap a piece of yarn around the bridge of the nose, cut and glue. Continue wrapping the yarn around the second lens and along the second arm. Cut and glue the yarn *(see photo 12)*.

Note: you can also buy ready-made dolls' spectacles.

7

8

9

10

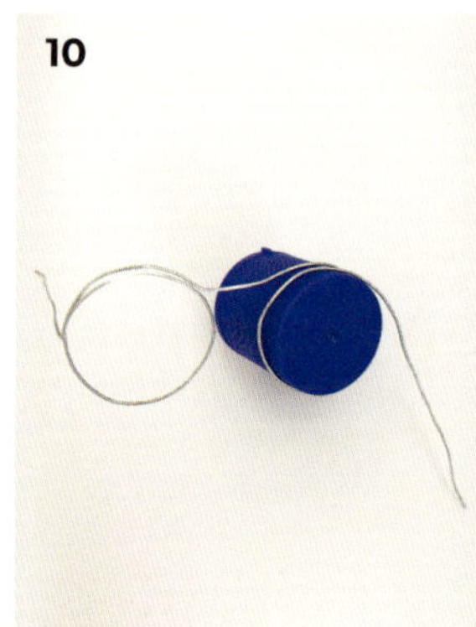

11

12

WHY NOT MAKE A FAMILY *just like yours?*

- By choosing from the skin and hair colours below:

Skin colours – DMC Natura Just Cotton:

Acanthe 81 | Gardenia 36 | Cinnamon 37 | Siena 41

Hair colours – Hobbii Diablo:

Caramel 15 | Honey 49 | Yellow Ochre 18 | Light Grey 04 | Black 09 | Rust 16 | Primrose 51

Or Hobbii Mohair Delight:

Cinnamon 34 | Nougat 04 | Titanium Grey 05 | Black 08 | Burnt Ochre 22 | Ginger 23

Or DMC Natura Just Cotton:

Siena 41 | Tropic Brown 22 | Black 11 | Grey 121 | Silver Grey 09 | Sunflower 16 | Saffron 47

- **You can also swap the adults' clothes:** how about putting Mother in Father's jeans? And Grandma in Father's blazer with an edging worked in silver yarn? How about swapping out Father's trousers for Bermuda shorts simply by shortening the legs?
- **Try varying the children's clothes** (you will find suggested variations in the respective instructions for each garment).
- …**Or make new pairs of spectacles.**

Note: if you are crocheting hair using cotton yarn, use the same hook as the one used for the rest of the doll and not the one recommended for wool yarn. You will need to adapt the length of the hairpiece, working one or two rows less (refer to the specific instructions for the project).

Now you can bring the family to life for the enjoyment of your loved ones!

Abbreviations and US equivalents of crochet terms can be found on page 12.

Crochet stitches

Techniques you need to know

Slip knot

Step 1: Put the hook behind the yarn and twist the hook as indicated by the arrow.
Step 2: Pinch the loop made with your thumb. Then wrap the yarn around the hook (= 1 yrh) as shown in the diagram.
Step 3: Draw the yarn around the hook through the loop.
Step 4: Pull the end of the yarn downwards to tighten the loop that you have just formed.

①

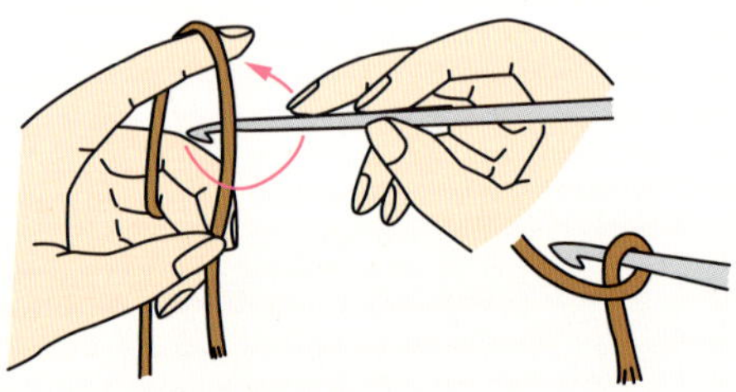

②

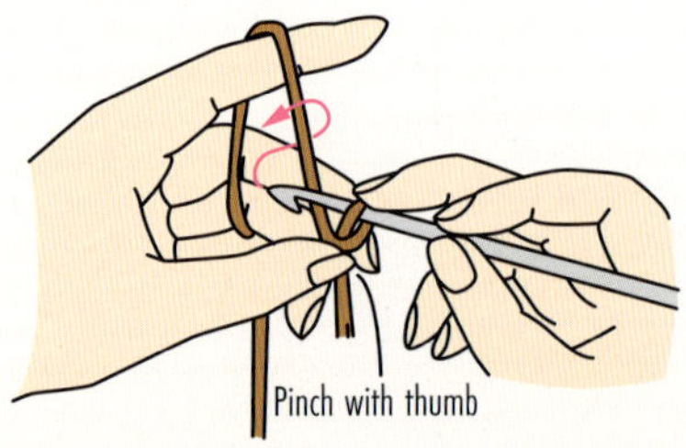

③

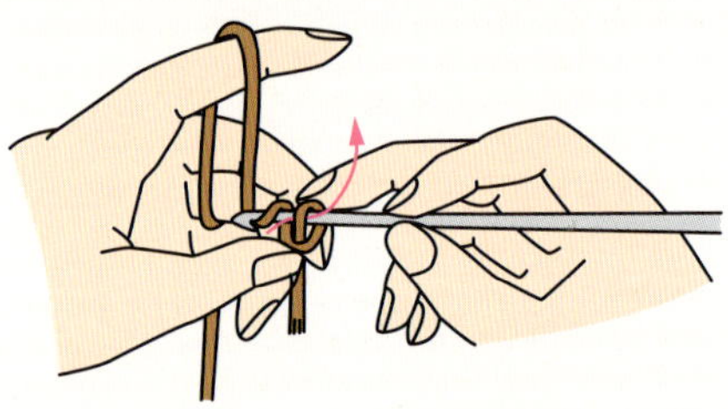

④

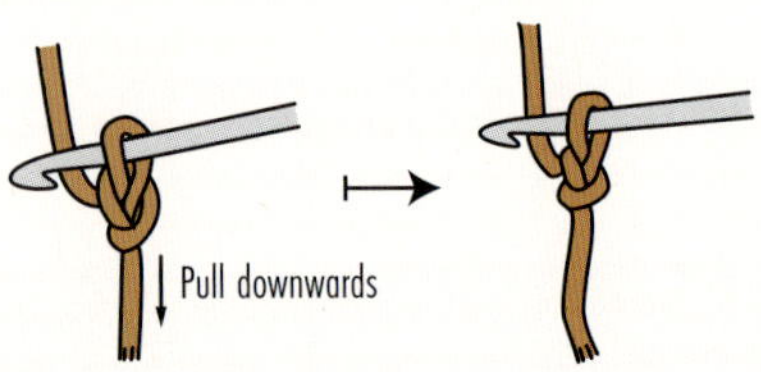

Magic ring (MR)

Step 1: Wrap the yarn twice around your forefinger and insert the hook through the loops. Wrap the ball end of the yarn around the hook, then pull it through the ring, as shown in the diagram. One loop on the hook.
Step 2: Wrap the yarn around the hook once and draw the yarn through the loops. You have made a magic ring.

Note: after you have worked around it once or twice, pull on the tail to draw the ring closed.

① ②

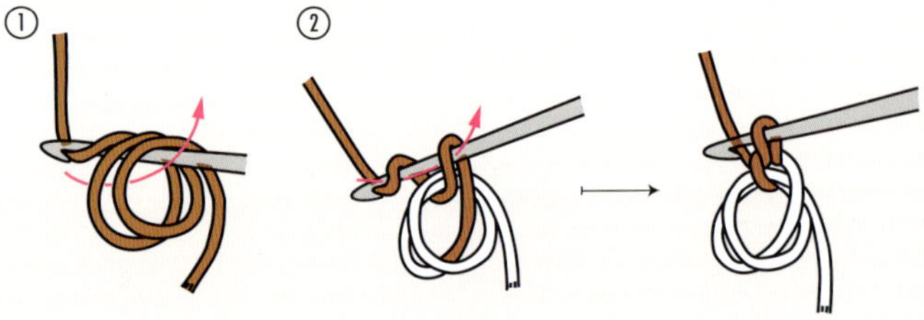

Chain stitch (ch)

Step 1: Wrap the yarn around the hook, picking up the yarn as indicated by the arrow.
Step 2: Draw the yarn through the starting loop to form the first chain stitch.
Step 3: Yarn round hook and pull the yarn through to form the second chain stitch.
Step 4: Repeat step 3.

①

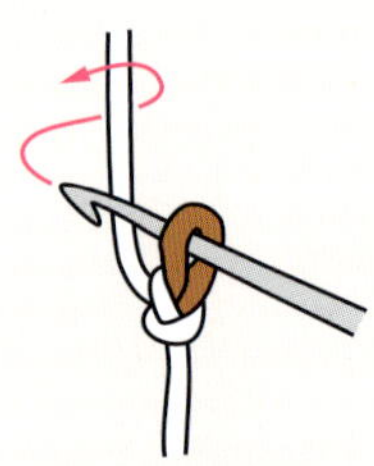

②

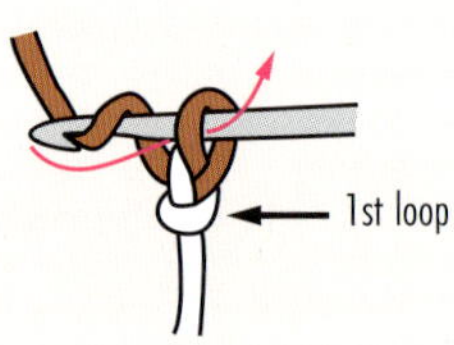

③

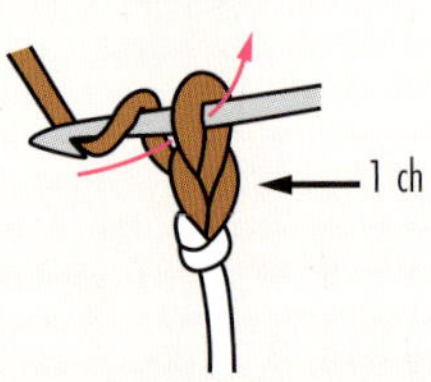

④

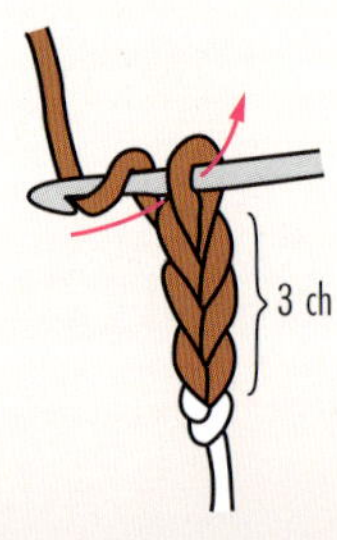

Slip stitch (sl st)

Step 1: At the start of the row, insert the hook into the first stitch as indicated by the arrow.
Step 2: Wrap the yarn around the hook and draw it through the stitch and the loop on the hook as indicated by the arrow.
Step 3: Insert the hook through the second stitch according to the arrow.
Step 4: Continue in the same way, drawing through both the stitch and the loop on the hook.

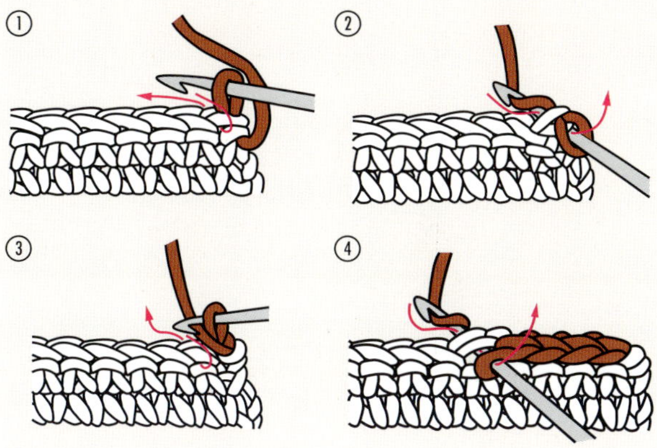

Double crochet (dc)

Step 1: Work one chain stitch to turn, then insert the hook into the next chain or stitch as shown on the diagram.
Step 2: Wrap the yarn around the hook and draw it through the chain or stitch as indicated by the arrow. Two loops on the hook.
Step 3: Wrap the yarn around the hook and draw it through the loops on the hook.
Step 4: You have worked a double crochet. Repeat steps 1 to 3.
Step 5: To continue along the whole foundation chain or row, simply insert the hook into the next stitch then repeat steps 2 and 3.

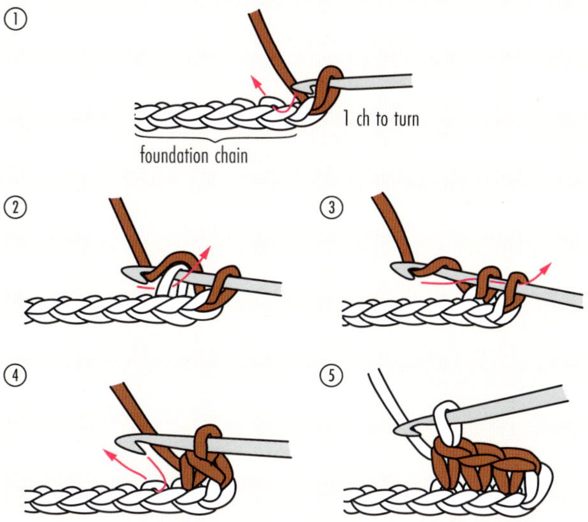

Treble (tr)

Step 1: Work three chain stitches at the start of a row in place of the first treble stitch (this counts as a stitch in your stitch count). Wrap the yarn around the hook and insert the hook into the fifth chain from the hook.
Step 2: Wrap the yarn around the hook and draw the yarn through the stitch according to the arrow. Three loops on the hook.
Step 3: Wrap the yarn around the hook and draw the yarn through two loops on the hook; you need only work three chains at the beginning of row 1.
Step 4: Wrap the yarn around the hook and draw the yarn through the two loops remaining on the hook. To continue along the whole foundation chain or row, simply wrap the yarn around the hook, insert the hook into the next stitch, then repeat steps 2 to 4.

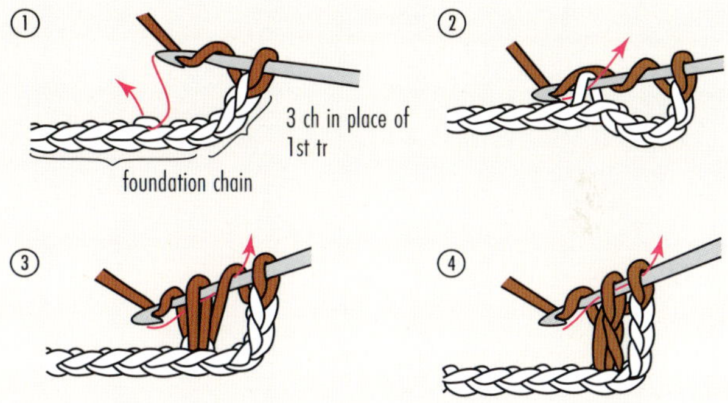

Half-treble (htr)

Step 1: Work two chain stitches in place of the first half-treble stitch (this counts as a stitch in your stitch count). Wrap the yarn around the hook before inserting the hook in the fourth chain stitch from the hook.
Step 2: Wrap the yarn around the hook and draw the yarn through the stitch. Three loops on the hook. Wrap the yarn around the hook again and draw the yarn through all the loops on the hook.
Step 3: You have worked a half-treble. Repeat steps 1 and 2 to work the rest of the row, omitting the two chains.

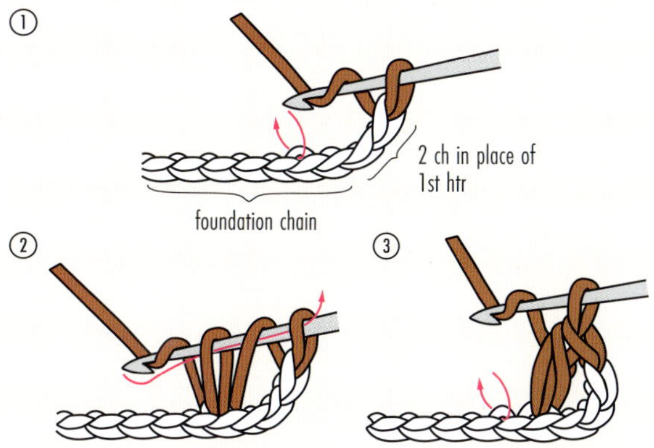

Double treble (dtr)

Step 1: Work four chain stitches at the beginning of the row in place of the first double treble stitch (this counts as a stitch in your stitch count), then wrap the yarn around the hook twice and insert the hook into the sixth chain from the hook.
Step 2: Wrap the yarn around the hook and draw the yarn through the stitch. Four loops on the hook. Wrap the yarn round the hook again and draw the yarn through two loops. Three loops on the hook.
Step 3: Wrap the yarn around the hook again and draw the yarn through two loops. Two loops on the hook.
Step 4: Wrap the yarn around the hook and draw yarn through the last two loops on the hook.
Step 5: You have worked a double treble. Repeat steps 1 to 4 to work the rest of the row, omitting the first chains.

①

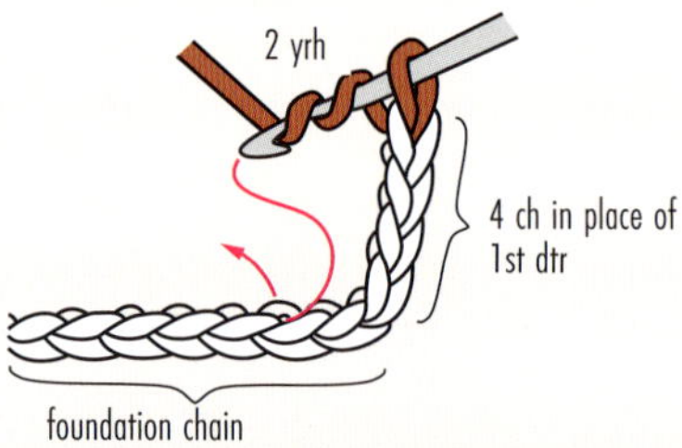

②

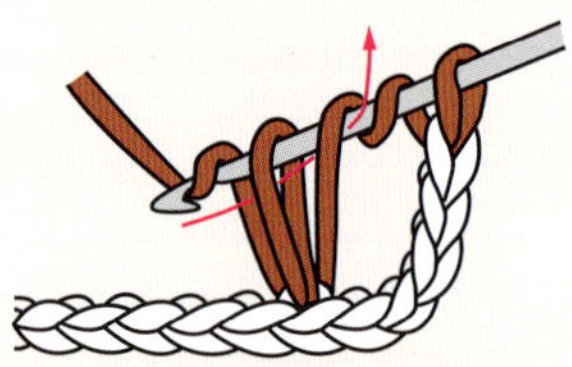

③

④

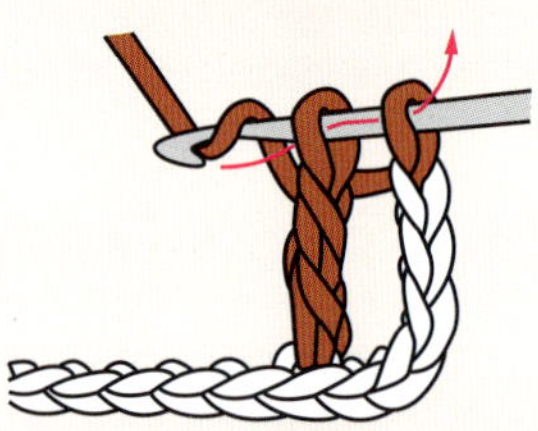

⑤

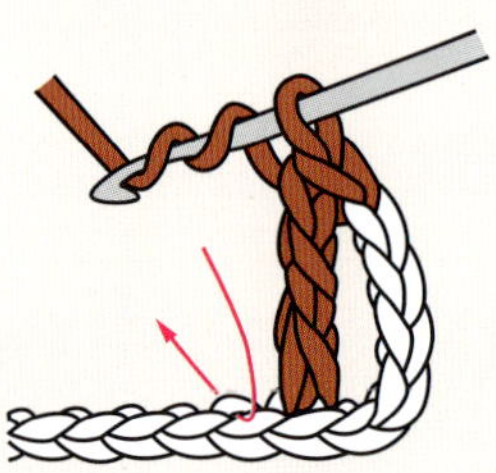

Increasing (in double crochet, 2 dc in next st)

Step 1: Insert the hook in the stitch in which the preceding double crochet was worked. Wrap the yarn around the hook.
Step 2: Draw the yarn through the stitch, wrap the yarn around the hook and draw through the two loops on the hook.
Step 3: You have worked an increase.

Note: the principle is the same for an increase when you are working in trebles (= two trebles in the same stitch) or half-trebles (= two half-trebles in the same stitch).

①

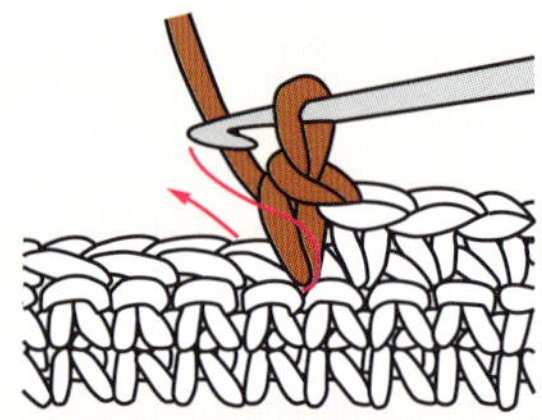

②

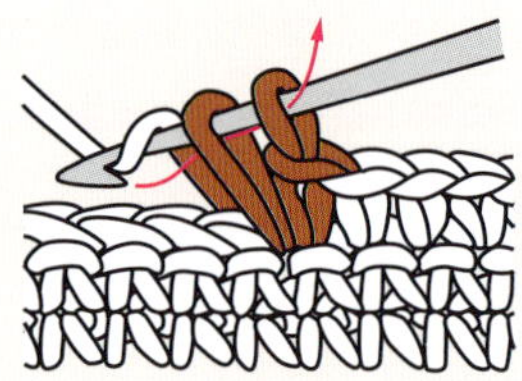

③

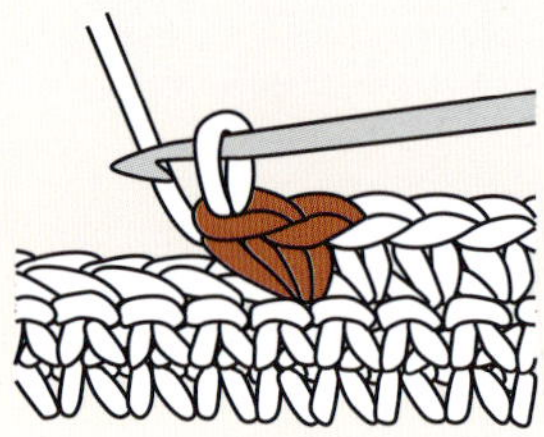

Decreasing (in double crochet, dc2tog)

Step 1: Insert the hook in the stitch, wrap the yarn around the hook, then draw the yarn through the stitch. Rep on the next stitch (= two incomplete double crochets).
Step 2: Wrap the yarn around the hook and draw the yarn through all loops on the hook.
Step 3: You have worked a decrease (there is one less double crochet stitch).

Note: for decreases in half-trebles, the principle is similar, but for step 1, wrap the yarn around the hook each time before inserting the hook in the stitches.

①

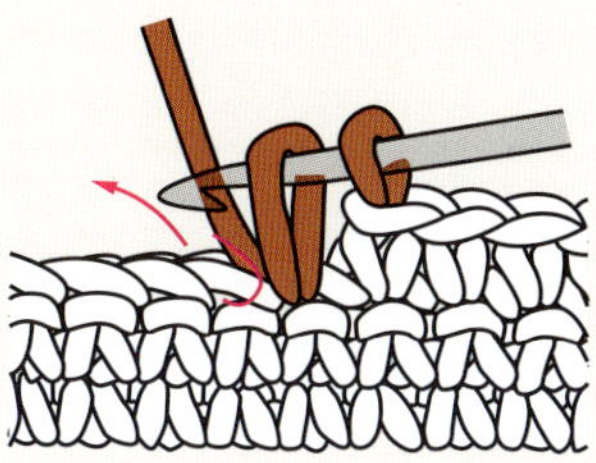

②

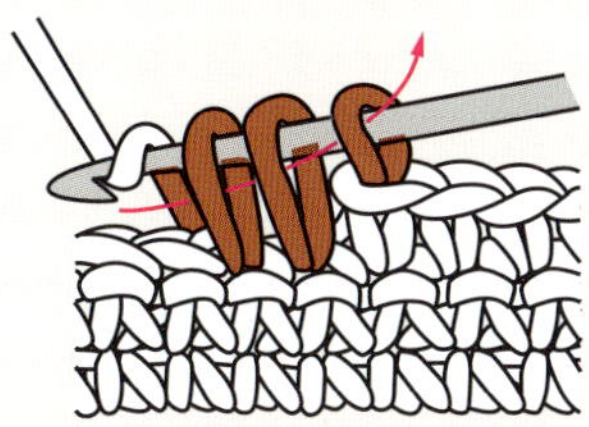

③

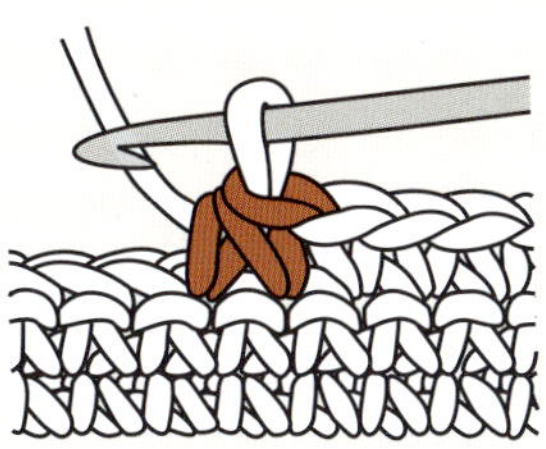

Front-post half-treble

Step 1: Wrap the yarn around the hook, then insert the hook horizontally (from right to left, from front to back) around the post of the stitch of the previous row/round.
Step 2: Wrap the yarn around the hook and draw it through the stitch, according to the arrow.
Step 3: Wrap the yarn around the hook and draw it through all the loops on the hook.
Step 4: You have worked a front-post half-treble.

Note: for a front-post treble, work step 1, then finish the treble as normal.

①

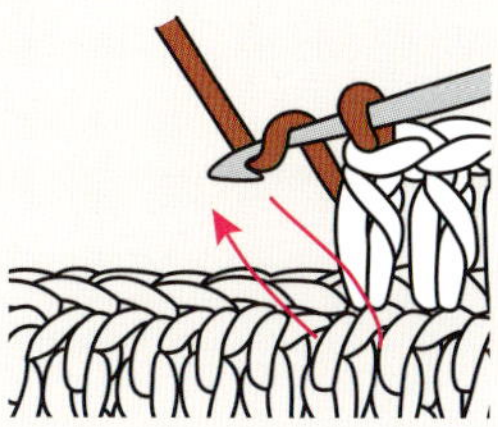

②

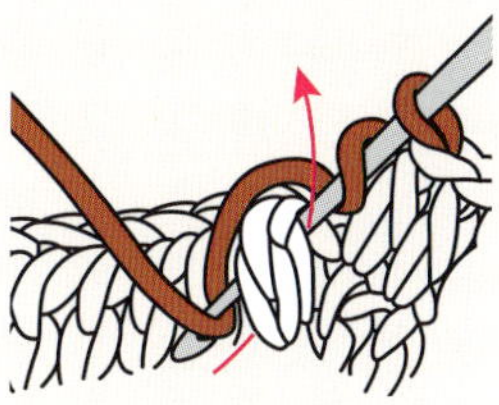

③

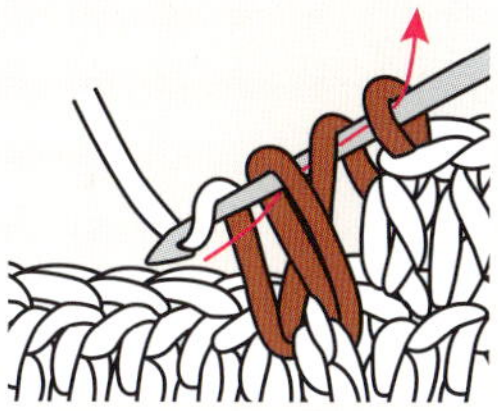

④

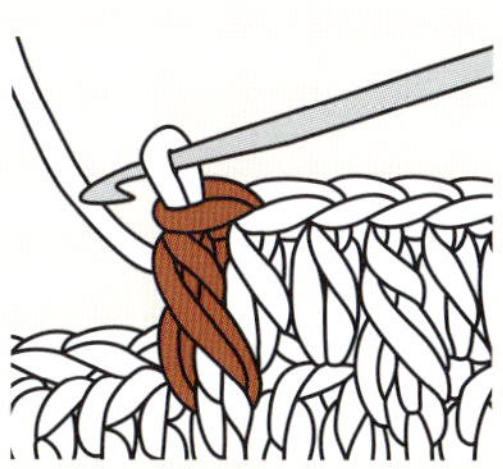

Back-post half-treble

Step 1: Wrap the yarn around the hook, then insert the hook horizontally (from right to left, from back to front) around the post of the stitch of the previous row/round.
Step 2: Wrap the yarn around the hook and draw it through all the loops on the hook.
Step 3: You have worked a back-post half-treble.

①
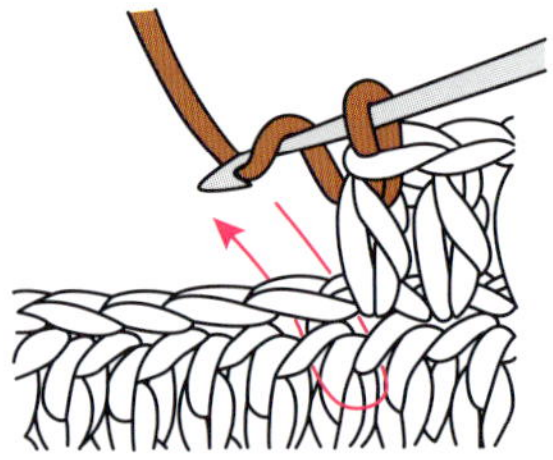

②
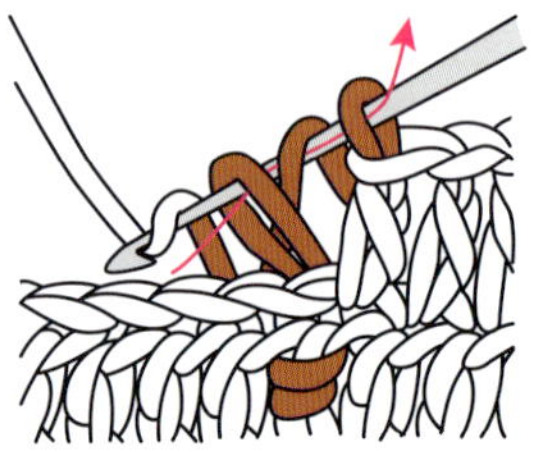

③
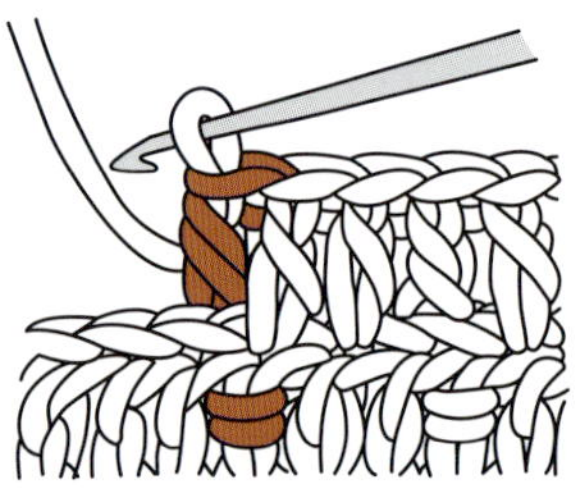

3-treble bobble

Step 1: Wrap the yarn around the hook, then insert the hook through the chain stitch marked by the arrow.
Step 2: Wrap the yarn around the hook, then draw the yarn through the stitch.
Step 3: Wrap the yarn around the hook, then draw it through two loops on the hook (incomplete treble). Repeat steps 1 to 3 twice more (inserting the hook in the same stitch) to obtain three incomplete trebles.
Step 4: Wrap the yarn around the hook, then draw it through all the loops on the hook.

①
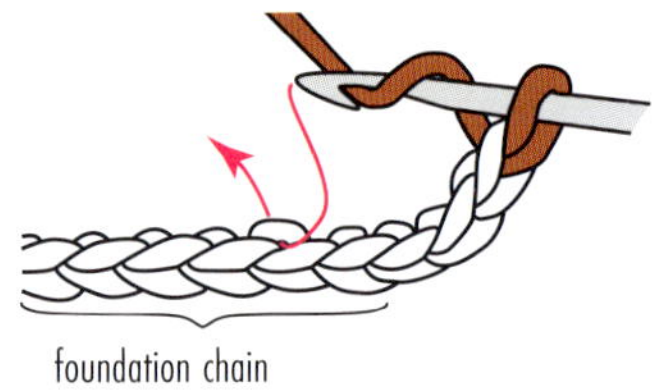

②
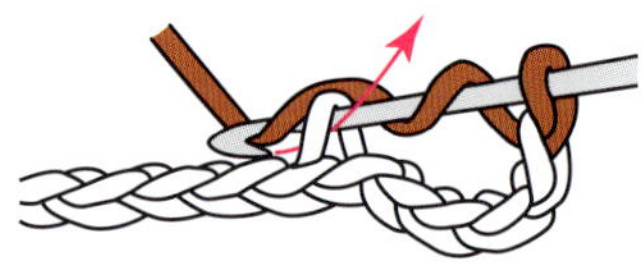

③
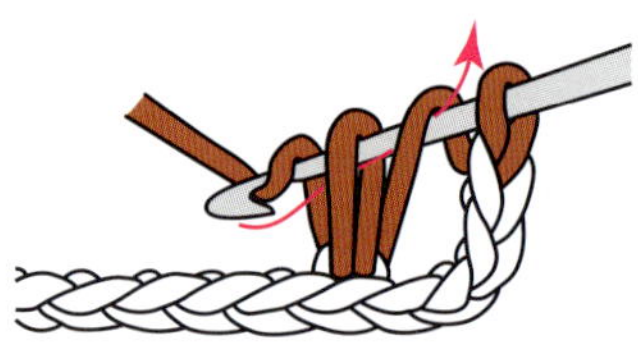

④
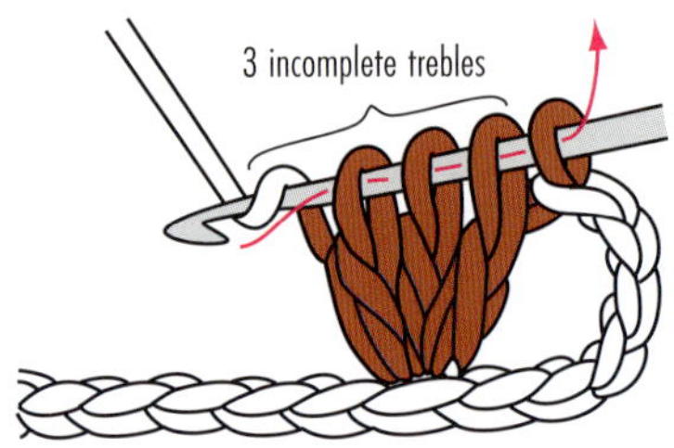

Front loop only (flo) and back loop only (blo)

The top of a stitch is made up of two loops, the nearest one (front loop: ①) and the furthest one (back loop: ②). If necessary, only insert the hook in the front or back loop of the stitch, without changing anything else about how you work the stitch.

①
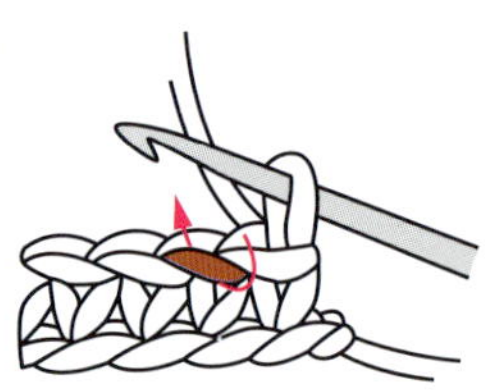

②
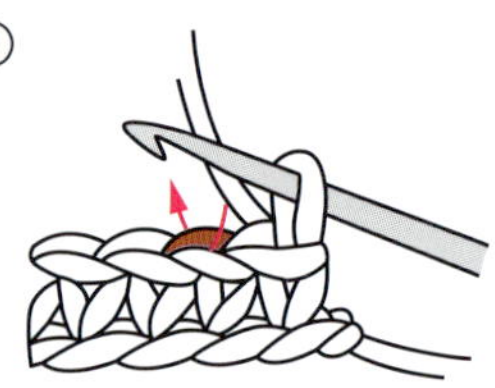

Embroidery

The basic stitches

French knot

Bring the needle up at point 1. Wrap the thread around the needle two or three times and hold in place with your left thumb. Reinsert the needle at point 2, close to point 1.

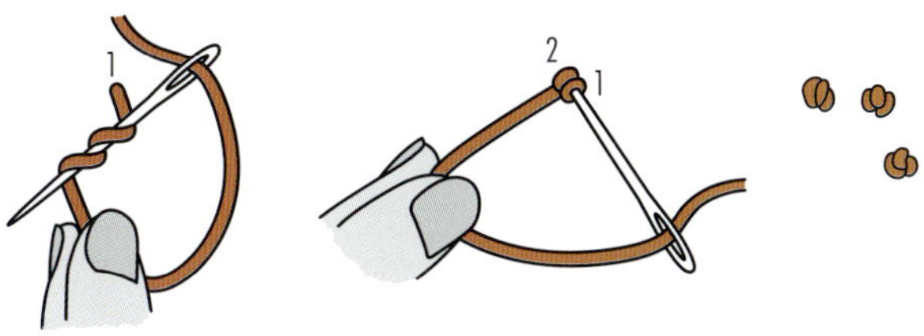

Straight stitch

Bring the needle up at point 1, then insert the needle at 2. If you wish to make a new stitch, bring up the needle at point 3. Work straight stitches closely together to make a satin stitch effect, which is used for eyes and noses.

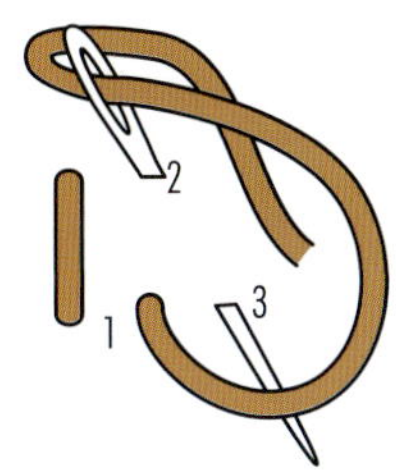

Backstitch

This stitch is worked from right to left. Bring the needle up at point 1, insert to the right at 2 and bring back up at 3 (the distance between 1 and 2 is the same as that between 3 and 1). Reinsert the needle at point 1, making sure that you do not split the thread of the previous stitch. The stitches should be neat and even.

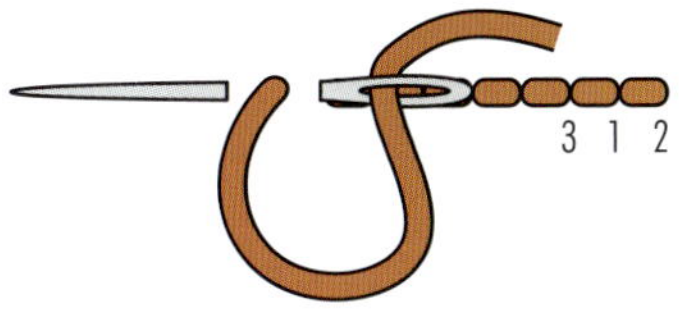

Chain stitch

Insert the needle at 1 and bring it out at 2, at a slight angle. Make sure that the yarn wraps around in a loop and under the needle. Then reinsert it inside the loop and bring it out again at 3. Repeat these steps, working evenly and making sure you do not pull too hard on the thread as you are forming the loops. Secure with a small stitch to finish.

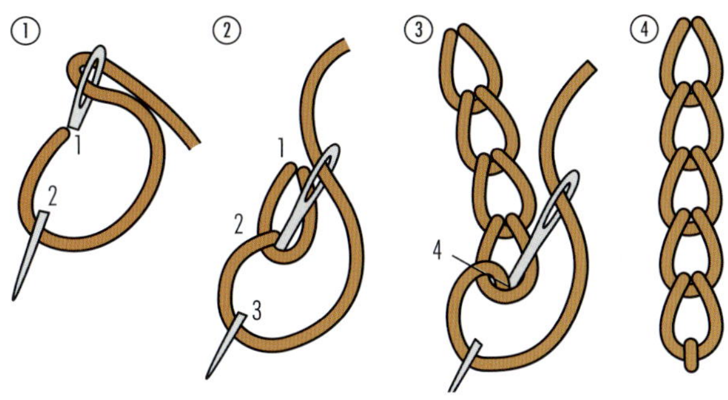

Lulu's family

Today is a great day – it is Susan's birthday and the whole family is busy preparing the perfect party: bunting, balloons, cake and flowers, not to mention sweets and presents.

Dolls

The Parents

Clementine and Anthony's eyes first met across the university lecture theatre. Shy smiles and furtive glances in the corridors slowly led to the discovery of a shared passion for literature. Many long evenings of discussion followed and they were soon spending hours cuddled up together reading. Clementine became a teacher after graduating with a degree in literature, while Anthony devoted himself to his passion, photography. As close as ever, the arrival of their four children completed their happy story.

Clementine

THE MOTHER

Finished height: 27cm (10½in)

You will need

DMC Natura Just Cotton (4-ply/fingering) yarn, 50g/1¾oz/155m/170yd, in (R), (F), (Y), (BB), (E), (A) and a little of (N), (Z), (X), (C), (L), (G)
Hobbii Diablo (1–3-ply/lace weight) yarn, 50g/1¾oz/225m/246yd, in (FF), for the hair (it is also possible to use DMC Natura Just Cotton – see page 17)

Black embroidery thread
Fine wire (for the stalks of the flowers)
2.25mm (UK 13, US B1) crochet hook, 3mm (UK 11, US 2/3) crochet hook for the hair
Basic tools and materials (see pages 10–12)

Special stitch:
3-treble bobble (3 tr for thumbs) (see page 22)

Making the doll

Note: unless stated otherwise, always work in spiral rounds using a 2.25mm (UK 13, US B1) crochet hook.

Body

Note: start with the legs.

Leg (make two)

Use yarns (A) and (R). Stuff the legs as your work progresses. Start with yarn (A).

Round 1: 6 dc into a MR (6 sts).
Round 2: 2 dc in each st around (12 sts).
Round 3: 1 dc in each st around (12 sts).
Rounds 4 and 5: 2 dc in the next st, 5 dc, dc2tog, 4 dc (12 sts).
Round 6: 1 dc, 2 dc in the next st, 5 dc, dc2tog, 3 dc (12 sts).
Rounds 7 and 8: 2 dc, 2 dc in the next st, 4 dc, dc2tog, 3 dc (12 sts).
Rounds 9 and 10: 2 dc, 2 dc in the next st, 4 dc, 2 dc in the next st, 3 dc (12 sts).
Rounds 11–14: 1 dc in each st around (12 sts).
Round 15: 3 dc, 2 dc in the next st, 8 dc (13 sts).
Rounds 16 and 17: 1 dc in each st around (13 sts).
Round 18: 4 dc, 2 dc in the next st, 8 dc (14 sts).
Rounds 19 and 20: 1 dc in each st around (14 sts).
Round 21: 5 dc, 2 dc in the next st, 8 dc (15 sts).
Rounds 22–24: 1 dc in each st around (15 sts).
Round 25: (3 dc, dc2tog) three times (12 sts).
Rounds 26 and 27: 1 dc in each st around (12 sts).
Round 28: 3 dc, 2 dc in the next st, 5 dc, 2 dc in the next st, 2 dc (14 sts).
Round 29: 1 dc in each st around (14 sts).
Round 30: 4 dc, 2 dc in the next st, 6 dc, 2 dc in the next st, 2 dc (16 sts).
Rounds 31 and 32: 1 dc in each st around (16 sts).
Round 33: (6 dc, 2 dc in the next st) twice, 2 dc (18 sts).
Rounds 34–37: 1 dc in each st around (18 sts).
Round 38: (8 dc, 2 dc in the next st) twice (20 sts).
Rounds 39 and 40: 1 dc in each st around (20 sts).
Finish with 1 sl st.

Cut yarn and weave in end.

Finish stuffing.

1

2

Crochet second leg in same way as far as round 40. Work 7 or 8 additional dc to reach inside of leg *(see photo 1)*, join yarn (R) at the end of the last dc and continue as follows:

Body

Use yarns (R), (A) and (BB). Stuff the body as you go. Lay the two legs side by side, toes up and with the second leg still on the hook: 1 ch and join to first leg with 1 dc (counted as first dc of round).

Round 1: 1 dc in each st around first leg, 1 dc in chain, 1 dc in each st around the other leg and 1 dc on other side of chain (20 + 1 + 20 + 1 = 42 sts) *(see photo 2)*. Place stitch marker here (it will be on doll's front).
Rounds 2–5: 1 dc in each st around (42 sts).
Round 6: 10 dc, dc2tog, 18 dc, dc2tog, 10 dc (40 sts).
Round 7: 1 dc in each st around (40 sts).
Round 8: 9 dc, dc2tog, 18 dc, dc2tog, 9 dc (38 sts).
Round 9: 28 dc, changing to yarn (A) on last yrh (28 sts). Move stitch marker.
Round 10: 1 dc in blo of each st around (38 sts).
Round 11: dc2tog, 18 dc, dc2tog, 16 dc (36 sts), changing to yarn (R) on last yrh to make the sweater (fasten off yarn (A)) *(see photo 3)*.

***Note:** always change yarn colour on last yrh of the round in question. Leave the unused yarn hanging on the wrong side of the work, continue with the new colour, then pick up the waiting yarn at the stated round.*

Round 12: 1 dc in each st around (36 sts).
Round 13: (dc2tog, 16 dc) twice (34 sts). Continue using yarn (BB).
Round 14: 1 dc in each st around (34 sts). Continue using yarn (R).
Rounds 15 and 16: 1 dc in each st around (34 sts); work another 1 dc and move the stitch marker to centre the joins on the side. Continue using yarn (BB).
Round 17: 1 dc in each st around (34 sts). Continue using yarn (R).
Round 18: 1 dc in each st around (34 sts).
Round 19: 16 dc, dc2tog, 14 dc, dc2tog (32 sts); work 1 dc (new start of round). Continue using yarn (BB).
Round 20: 1 dc in each st around (32 sts). Continue using yarn (R).
Round 21: 1 dc in each st around (32 sts).
Round 22: (6 dc, dc2tog) four times (28 sts). Continue using yarn (BB).
Round 23: 1 dc in each st around (28 sts). Continue using yarn (R).
Round 24: (5 dc, dc2tog) four times (24 sts), changing to yarn (A) on last yrh. Cut yarn and weave in ends of yarns (R) and (BB).
Round 25: 1 dc in blo of each st around (24 sts).
Round 26: (4 dc, dc2tog) four times (20 sts).

3

4

5

Round 27: (3 dc, dc2tog) four times (16 sts).
Round 28: (2 dc, dc2tog) four times (12 sts) *(see photo 4)*.

***Note:** this is the start of the 'tube' on which the head will be fixed.*

Rounds 29–40: 1 dc in each st around (12 sts). Finish stuffing.
Round 41: 6 dc2tog (6 sts). Sew up the opening with a darning needle, leaving around 30cm (12in) of yarn to sew the head on at a later stage.

***Note:** to make the neck more stable, slip a pipe cleaner (chenille stick) into the opening (see photo 5).*

Project continues overleaf

Arm (make two)

Crocheted separately using yarns (A), (R) and (BB) *(see photo 6)*.

Right arm

Start with yarn (A).
Round 1: 5 dc into a MR (5 sts).
Round 2: 2 dc in each st around (10 sts).
Rounds 3–5: 1 dc in each st around (10 sts).
Round 6: 1 dc, 1 bobble st (thumb), 8 dc (10 sts).
Round 7: 1 dc in each st around (10 sts).
Round 8: 1 dc, dc2tog, 3 dc, dc2tog, 2 dc (8 sts).
Rounds 9–11: 1 dc in each st around (8 sts).
Stuff hand lightly (using a wooden skewer or crochet hook handle to help). Continue using yarn (R). to start the stripes.

Note: always change yarn colour on the last yrh of the round in question. Leave the unused yarn hanging on the wrong side of the work, continue with the new colour, then pick up the waiting yarn at the stated round.

Rounds 12 and 13: 1 dc in each st around (8sts); work another 1 dc and move the stitch marker to centre the joins on the back of the arm. Continue using yarn (BB).
Round 14: 7 dc, 2 dc in the next st (9 sts). Continue using yarn (R).
Rounds 15 and 16: 1 dc in each st around (9 sts). Continue using yarn (BB).
Round 17: 8 dc, 2 dc in the next st (10 sts). Continue using yarn (R).
Rounds 18 and 19: 1 dc in each st around (10 sts). Continue using yarn (BB).
Round 20: 1 dc in each st around (10 sts). Continue using yarn (R).
Rounds 21 and 22: 1 dc in each st around (10 sts); 1 dc (new start of row). Continue using yarn (BB).
Round 23: 1 dc in each st around (10 sts). Continue using yarn (R).
Rounds 24 and 25: 1 dc in each st around (10 sts). 1 dc (new start of row). Continue using yarn (BB).
Round 26: 1 dc in each st around (10 sts). Continue using yarn (R). Cut yarn (BB) and weave in end.
Round 27: 1 dc in each st around (10 sts).
Round 28: 1 dc in each of the next 8 or 9 sts in order to centre the joins on the back of the arm and position the thumb against the side of the body.
Pinch top of arm together and sew up with 4 dc into sts on both sides at same time. Cut, leaving sufficient yarn for making up.

6

7

Left arm

Start with yarn (A).
Round 1: 5 dc into a MR (5 sts).
Round 2: 2 dc in each st around (10 sts).
Rounds 3–5: 1 dc in each st around (10 sts).
Round 6: 6 dc, 1 bobble st (thumb), 3 dc (10 sts).
Round 7: 1 dc in each st around (10 sts).
Round 8: 1 dc, dc2tog, 3 dc, dc2tog, 2 dc (8 sts).
Rounds 9–11: 1 dc in each st around (8 sts). Stuff hand lightly.
Rounds 12–28: rep as for the right arm (including alternating the colours). Cut, leaving sufficient yarn for making up.
Sew the arms on either side of the body, at round 25, ensuring the thumbs are facing in the right direction *(see photo 7)*.

Head

Use yarn (A).
Round 1: 6 dc into a MR (6 sts).
Round 2: 2 dc in each st around (12 sts).
Round 3: (1 dc, 2 dc in the next st) six times (18 sts).
Round 4: (2 dc, 2 dc in the next st) six times (24 sts).
Round 5: (3 dc, 2 dc in the next st) six times (30 sts).
Round 6: (4 dc, 2 dc in the next st) six times (36 sts).
Round 7: (5 dc, 2 dc in the next st) six times (42 sts).
Round 8: (6 dc, 2 dc in the next st) six times (48 sts).
Round 9: (11 dc, 2 dc in the next st) four times (52 sts).
Rounds 10–20: 1 dc in each st around (52 sts).
Round 21: (11 dc, dc2tog) four times (48 sts).
Round 22: 1 dc in each st around (48 sts).
Round 23: 3 dc, dc2tog, (6 dc, dc2tog) five times, 3 dc (42 sts). Start stuffing and continue as you go.
Round 24: (5 dc, dc2tog) six times (36 sts).
Round 25: 2 dc, dc2tog, (4 dc, dc2tog) five times, 2 dc (30 sts).
Round 26: (3 dc, dc2tog) six times (24 sts).
Round 27: 1 dc, dc2tog, (2 dc, dc2tog) five times, 1 dc (18 sts).
Round 28: (1 dc, dc2tog) six times (12 sts).
Finish round with 1 sl st and leave a long tail of yarn for sewing up.
Finish stuffing.

Prepare the opening into which the 'tube' will be inserted, using the handle of the crochet hook to help.

Thread a long needle with the tail of yarn from the 'tube' and pass it up through the opening in the head, bringing it out on top. Use this yarn to guide the head on to the tube until it reaches round 31. This will make it more stable. Knot yarn at top of head and weave in end. Sew the head to the neck, passing the needle through the loops of the sts of the last round of the head and between the sts of the neck. Cut yarn and weave in end *(see photos 8 to 10)*.

8

9

10

Project continues overleaf

Hair

Use Hobbii Diablo yarn (FF) – 3mm (UK 11, US 2/3) crochet hook.

Note: it is also possible to use cotton yarn (see page 17).

Hairpiece

Round 1: 6 dc into a MR (6 sts).
Round 2: 2 dc in each st around (12 sts).
Round 3: (1 dc, 2 dc in the next st) six times (18 sts).
Round 4: (2 dc, 2 dc in the next st) six times (24 sts).
Round 5: (3 dc, 2 dc in the next st) six times (30 sts).
Round 6: (4 dc, 2 dc in the next st) six times (36 sts).
Round 7: (5 dc, 2 dc in the next st) six times (42 sts).
Round 8: (6 dc, 2 dc in the next st) six times (48 sts).
Round 9: (11 dc, 2 dc in the next st) four times (52 sts).
Rounds 10–25: 1 dc in each st around (52 sts). (The number of rounds can be adapted depending on the yarn used and your own crocheting style. Try the hairpiece before you work the last round.)

Do not fasten off but continue with the individual strands *(see photo 11)*; crochet 1 sl st then 24 ch, sk 22 sts and secure the strand with 1 sl st into the twenty-third st.

Work 24 ch again and secure the strand in the starting sl st. Rep these steps once more to form three strands. Work 20 ch, skip 18 sts and secure the strand on the other side of the hairpiece with 1 sl st in the nineteenth st. Leave a long tail of yarn for sewing up. Adjust the hairpiece on the head and hold in place with pins *(see photo 12)*.

Sew on the hairpiece, following the sts of the last round.

Cut yarn and weave in end.

Knot or embroider a few strands on the forehead.

> ***Tip***
> ***Gently brush the hair with a little metal brush to make the fibres stand out.***

Bun

Round 1: 6 dc into a MR (6 sts).
Round 2: 2 dc in each st around (12 sts).
Round 3: (1 dc, 2 dc in the next st) six times (18 sts).
Round 4: (2 dc, 2 dc in the next st) six times (24 sts).
Round 5: (3 dc, 2 dc in the next st) six times (30 sts).
Round 6: (4 dc, 2 dc in the next st) six times (36 sts).
Rounds 7–11: 1 dc in each st around (36 sts).
Round 12: (4 dc, dc2tog) six times (30 sts).
Round 13: (3 dc, dc2tog) six times (24 sts).

Without fastening off, 1 sl st into next st, then work 80 ch to form a long braid to wrap around the bun. Thread the yarn through the loop to secure.

Stuff the bun lightly then sew to the head.

Wrap the braid around 3 times, allowing a few strands to escape *(see photos 13 to 14)*.

11

12

13

14

Embroider the eyes in black embroidery thread at round 19 (tenth round from the bottom of the head), spaced 9 sts apart. For a healthy glow, add a little colour to the cheeks using a piece of cloth coloured with red crayon *(see photo 15)*.

Skirt

Use yarn (Y).

Round 1: work 42 ch. Join with 1 dc into first ch (counts as first st of round), ensuring that the chain is not twisted) and work 1 dc in each st around (42 sts).
Rounds 2–5: 1 dc in each st around (42 sts) *(see photo 16)*.
Round 6: (13 dc, 3 dc in the next st) twice (45 sts).
Rounds 7 and 8: 1 dc in each st around (45 sts).
Round 9: (14 dc, 2 dc in the next st) three times (48 sts).
Rounds 10–13: 1 dc in each st around (48 sts).
Round 14: (7 dc, 2 dc in the next st) six times (54 sts).
Rounds 15 and 16: 1 dc in each st around (54 sts).
Round 17: (8 dc, 2 dc in the next st) six times (60 sts).
Round 18: 1 dc in each st around (60 sts).
Round 19: 1 sl st, 1 ch (counts as first htr), then 2 htr in each st around (120 sts). Finish with 1 sl st into starting ch. Cut yarn and weave in end.

Belt

Use yarn (BB).

Join the yarn in first st of round 1 and work 1 dc in each st around (42 sts). Finish with 1 sl st, then cut yarn and weave in end *(see photo 17)*.

Ballet pump (make two)

Use yarns (E) and (BB). Start with the sole in yarn (E). Work 8 ch *(see photo 18)*.

Note: sts will be crocheted on both sides of chain.

Round 1: starting in second ch from hook, 2 dc in the next st, 5 dc, 4 dc in first of 8 ch; continue on other side. 5 dc, 2 dc in the next st (18 sts).
Round 2: 2 dc in the next st, 6 dc, 2 dc in the next 4 sts, 6 dc, 2 dc in the next st (24 sts).
Round 3: 1 dc in each st around (24 sts), changing to yarn (BB) on last yrh.
Round 4: 8 dc, 8 htr, 8 dc (24 sts).
Round 5: 9 dc, 8 htr in the next st, 7 dc (24 sts).
Round 6: 9 dc, 4 dc2tog, 7 dc (20 sts).
Round 7: 9 dc, 2 dc2tog, 7 dc (18 sts).
Finish with 1 sl st.

Fasten off and weave in ends.

15

16

17

18

Project continues overleaf

Making the accessories (see photo 19)

Net bag

Use yarn (F).

Start with the first part of the top of the bag.

Row 1: work 10 ch. Start in second ch from hook, 1 dc in each ch across (9 sts).

Rows 2 and 3: turn, 1 ch, 1 dc in each st across (9 sts). Then start the first loops of the mesh pattern.

Row 4: turn, *4 ch, secure with 1 dc in next st, rep from * to end of row. There are 8 loops along the top of the bag.

Rows 5–14: turn, *5 ch, secure with 1 dc in loop of previous row, rep from * to end of row *(see photo 20)*.

Row 15: turn, 4 ch, secure with 1 dc in loop of previous round. Rep to end of row *(see photo 21)*.

Then work the second part of the top of the bag.

Row 16: turn, 2 ch, then 1 dc in each loop to end (10 sts) *(see photo 22)*.

Row 17: turn, 1 ch, 1 dc in second st of previous round, 1 dc in each st to end (9 sts).

Row 18: turn, 1 ch, 1 dc in each st across (9 sts). Without fastening off, crochet the handles as follows: 25 ch and continue directly with the sides of the bag: 3 dc along the 3 rows of the rectangle, 1 dc in each of the 7 loops of the mesh pattern, 3 dc along the side of the second rectangle and 25 ch to form the second strap of the bag.

Work around the rectangle and mesh one more time (3 dc + 7 dc + 3 dc).

Finishing off: work sl st along the handle, down the side, along the second handle and the other side. Cut yarn and weave in ends *(see photo 23)*.

Bouquet

Little flowers

Use yarns (R), (G) and (L) and some wire for the stems.

(See 'Little flower' diagram, opposite.)

Make one or two of each colour.

Round 1: work (2 ch, 1 tr, 2 ch, 1 sl st) five times into a MR to form five petals.

Draw tight and knot ends together.

Slip an 8cm (3¼in) length of wire between 2 sts on the back of the flowers, bend the end to secure and hold in place with a few stitches using the remaining cotton thread.

Cut yarn and weave in ends *(see photo 24)*.

19

20

21

22

23

Main stem

Use yarn (N).

Round 1: 5 dc into a MR (5 sts).

Rounds 2–11: 1 dc in each st around (5 sts).

Cut yarn and weave in end.

Bunch all the flowers together and slip the stems into the crocheted cone.

Secure if necessary with a dab of glue or a few stitches *(see photo 25)*.

Apples

Use yarns (Z) and (C).

Crochet one in each colour.

Stuff apple as you go.

Round 1: 6 dc into a MR (6 sts).

Round 2: (1 dc, 2 dc in the next st) three times (9 sts).

Round 3: (2 dc, 2 dc in the next st) three times (12 sts).

Round 4: (1 dc, 2 dc in the next st) six times (18 sts).

Rounds 5–7: 1 dc in each st around (18 sts).

Round 8: (4 dc, dc2tog) three times (15 sts).

Round 9: 1 dc in each st around (15 sts).

Round 10: (3 dc, dc2tog) three times (12 sts).

Round 11: 6 dc2tog (6 sts).

Cut a length of yarn and sew up the opening with the darning needle, passing the needle through flo of the sts of the last round.

Weave in ends.

Stalk

Use yarn (X).

Work 4 ch, then starting in second ch from hook, crochet 3 sl st along the chain. Leave a long tail of yarn to sew the stalk to the top of the apple.

Insert the needle from top to bottom, bringing it out in the centre of the apple, then pull to draw in the two ends and bring the yarn back out at the stalk.

Knot yarn, weave in ends and cut *(see photo 26)*.

Baguette

Use yarn (E) and a bit of yarn (X). Stuff baguette as you go.

Round 1: 6 dc into a MR (6 sts).

Round 2: 1 dc in each st around (6 sts).

Round 3: (1 dc, 2 dc in the next st) three times (9 sts).

Rounds 4–23: 1 dc in each st around (9 sts).

Round 24: (1 dc, dc2tog) three times (6 sts). Cut a length of yarn and sew up the opening with the darning needle, passing the needle through flo of the sts of the last round.

Weave in end.

Embroider a few lines using yarn (X) on the front of the baguette.

Little flower

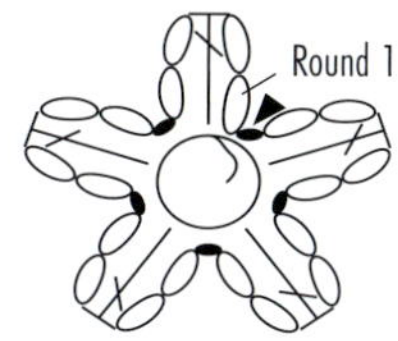

◄ **Fasten off.**

◯ **1 magic ring**

⊖ **1 chain stitch:** yrh, draw it through loop on hook.

- **1 slip stitch:** insert hook through first st, yrh and draw through st and loop on hook.

Ŧ **1 treble:** yrh, insert hook through first st, yrh and draw through st then (yrh, draw through two loops) twice.

24

25

26

Anthony

THE FATHER

Finished height: 28cm (11in)

You will need

DMC Natura Just Cotton (4-ply/fingering) yarn, 50g/1¾oz/155m/170yd, in (R), (P), (A), (BB), (E), (X), (S) and (AA) and a little of yarns (T), (F) and (O)

Hobbii Mohair Delight (DK/8-ply/light worsted) mohair yarn, 50g/1¾oz/150m/164yd, in (KK), for the hair (it is also possible to use Hobbii Diablo doubled or DMC Natura Just Cotton – see page 17)

Embroidery thread in red, dark brown (or black), white, beige

2.25mm (UK 13, US B1) crochet hook, 3.5mm (UK 9, US E4) crochet hook for the hair

Basic tools and materials (see pages 10–12)

Special stitch:

3-treble bobble (3 tr for thumbs) (see page 22)

Making the doll

Note: unless stated otherwise, always work in spiral rounds using a 2.25mm (UK 13, US B1) crochet hook.

Body

Note: start with the legs.

Leg (make two)

Use yarns (P), (A) and (R).
Stuff leg as you go.
Start using yarn (P).
Work 7 ch.

Note: sts will be crocheted on both sides of chain.

Round 1: starting in second ch from hook, 5 dc, 3 dc in last ch; continue on other side. 4 dc, 2 dc in the next st (14 sts).
Round 2: 2 dc in the next st, 4 dc, 2 dc in next 3 sts, 5 dc, 2 dc in the next st (19 sts).
Rounds 3 and 4: 1 dc in each st around (19 sts).
Round 5: 7 dc, 3 dc2tog, 6 dc (16 sts).
Round 6: 6 dc, 2 dc2tog, 6 dc (14 sts).
Round 7: 5 dc, 2 dc2tog, 5 dc (12 sts).
Rounds 8 and 9: 1 dc in each st around (12 sts), changing to yarn (A) on last yrh.
Round 10: 1 dc in blo of each st around (12 sts).
Round 11: 1 dc in each st around (12 sts) *(see photo 1)*.
Round 12: 2 dc in the next st, 11 dc (13 sts).
Rounds 13–16: 1 dc in each st around (13 sts).
Round 17: 2 dc, 2 dc in the next st, 10 dc (14 sts).
Rounds 18–22: 1 dc in each st around (14 sts).
Round 23: (dc2tog, 5 dc) twice (12 sts).
Rounds 24 and 25: 1 dc in each st around (12 sts).
Round 26: (2 dc in the next st, 5 dc) twice (14 sts).
Rounds 27 and 28: 1 dc in each st around (14 sts).
Round 29: 2 dc, 2 dc in the next st, 6 dc, 2 dc in the next st, 4 dc (16 sts).
Rounds 30 and 31: 1 dc in each st around (16 sts).
Round 32: 3 dc, 2 dc in the next st, 7 dc, 2 dc in the next st, 4 dc (18 sts).
Rounds 33–38: 1 dc in each st around (18 sts).
Round 39: 10 dc to reach back of leg, changing to yarn (R) on last yrh. Move stitch marker.
Round 40: 1 dc in each st around (18 sts). Finish with 1 sl st. Fasten off and weave in ends. Finish stuffing *(see photo 2)*.

Work second leg in same way until round 39, then change to yarn (R) and work 14 dc in new colour to reach inside of leg. Continue as follows:

1

2

3

Body

Use yarns (R), (P) and (A).
Stuff body as you go.
Lay the two legs side by side, toes up and with second leg still on the hook: 2 ch and join to first leg with 1 dc (counts as first dc of round).
Round 1: 1 dc in each of 18 sts of first leg, 1 dc in 2 sts of chain, 1 dc in each of 18 sts of the other leg and 1 dc in 2 sts on other side of chain (18 + 2 + 18 + 2 = 40 sts) *(see photo 3)*.
Place stitch marker here (it will be on doll's front).
Rounds 2–7: 1 dc in each st around (40 sts).
Round 8: 30 dc, changing to yarn (P) on last yrh (30 sts).
Move stitch marker.
Round 9: 1 dc in each st around (40 sts).
Round 10: (8 dc, dc2tog) four times (36 sts), changing to yarn (R) on last yrh.
Round 11: 1 dc in blo of each st around (36 sts).
Rounds 12–14: 1 dc in each st around (36 sts).
Round 15: (7 dc, dc2tog) four times (32 sts).
Rounds 16 and 17: 1 dc in each st around (32 sts).
Round 18: (6 dc, dc2tog) four times (28 sts).
Rounds 19 and 20: 1 dc in each st around (28 sts).
Round 21: (5 dc, dc2tog) four times (24 sts).
Rounds 22 and 23: 1 dc in each st around (24 sts).
Round 24: (4 dc, dc2tog) four times (20 sts).

Round 25: 1 dc in each st around (20 sts).
Round 26: (3 dc, dc2tog) four times (16 sts), changing to yarn (A) on last yrh.
Round 27: 1 dc in blo of each st around (16 sts) *(see photo 4)*.
Round 28: (6 dc, dc2tog) twice (14 sts).

Note: this is the start of the 'tube' on to which the head will be fixed.

Rounds 29–34: 1 dc in each st around (14 sts).
Round 35: (5 dc, dc2tog) twice (12 sts).
Rounds 36–39: 1 dc in each st around (12 sts). Finish stuffing.
Round 40: 6 dc2tog (6 sts).
Sew up the opening with a darning needle, leaving a 30cm (12in) tail of yarn to sew on the head at a later stage.

Note: to make the neck more stable, slip a pipe cleaner (chenille stick) into the opening (see photo 5).

Embroider a line around round 10 in backstitch, using red embroidery thread, to highlight the waist of the underpants.

Arm (make two)

Use yarns (A) and (R) *(see photo 6)*.
Start with yarn (A).
Round 1: 6 dc into a MR (6 sts).
Round 2: 2 dc in each st around (12 sts).
Rounds 3–5: 1 dc in each st around (12 sts).
Round 6: 5 dc, 1 bobble st (thumb), 6 dc (12 sts).
Round 7: 1 dc in each st around (12 sts).
Round 8: 2 dc, dc2tog, 5 dc, dc2tog, 1 dc (10 sts).
Rounds 9 and 10: 1 dc in each st around (10 sts). Stuff hand lightly using a wooden skewer or crochet hook handle to help.
Continue using yarn (R).
Rounds 11–20: 1 dc in each st around (10 sts).
Round 21: (4 dc, 2 dc in the next st) twice (12 sts).
Rounds 22–27: 1 dc in each st around (12 sts).
Pinch top of arm together, ensuring that the thumb points to the side of the body (add or sk 1 dc if necessary) and sew up with 5 dc into sts on both sides at same time.
Cut, leaving sufficient yarn for making up.
Sew the arms on either side of the body, at round 25, ensuring that the thumbs are facing in the right direction.

4
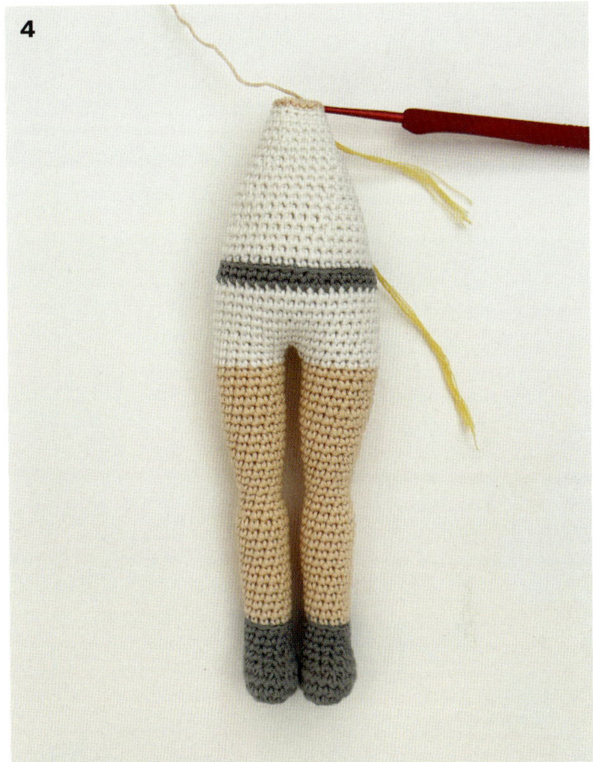

5

6

Project continues overleaf

Collar of polo shirt

Use yarn (R).

Row 1: work 17 ch, then starting in second ch from hook (2 dc in the next st, 2 dc) five times, 2 dc in the last st (22 sts).
Row 2: 1 ch, turn, 1 dc in each st across (22 sts).
Fasten off, leaving enough yarn to sew together.

Using the darning needle, weave the yarn through the sts along the edge, bringing out on first row, then sew the collar round the neck in flo of the sts of round 27. Fasten off and weave in ends.

Button placket

Embroider a band in chain stitch (using yarn (R)) over 4 sts on the body, between the points of the collar: 4 sts down and 4 sts back up. Weave in ends *(see photo 7)*.

Head

Use yarn (A).

Round 1: 6 dc into a MR (6 sts).
Round 2: 2 dc in each st around (12 sts).
Round 3: (1 dc, 2 dc in the next st) six times (18 sts).
Round 4: (2 dc, 2 dc in the next st) six times (24 sts).
Round 5: (3 dc, 2 dc in the next st) six times (30 sts).
Round 6: (4 dc, 2 dc in the next st) six times (36 sts).
Round 7: (5 dc, 2 dc in the next st) six times (42 sts).
Round 8: (6 dc, 2 dc in the next st) six times (48 sts).
Round 9: (11 dc, 2 dc in the next st) four times (52 sts).
Rounds 10–20: 1 dc in each st around (52 sts).
Round 21: (11 dc, dc2tog) four times (48 sts).
Round 22: 1 dc in each st around (48 sts).
Round 23: 3 dc, dc2tog, (6 dc, dc2tog) five times, 3 dc (42 sts). Start stuffing and continue as you go.
Round 24: (5 dc, dc2tog) six times (36 sts).
Round 25: 2 dc, dc2tog, (4 dc, dc2tog) five times, 2 dc (30 sts).
Round 26: (3 dc, dc2tog) six times (24 sts).
Round 27: 1 dc, dc2tog, (2 dc, dc2tog) five times, 1 dc (18 sts).
Round 28: (2 dc, dc2tog) four times, 2 dc (14 sts).
Join the round with 1 sl st and leave a long tail of yarn for sewing up *(see photo 8)*.

Finish stuffing.

Prepare the opening into which the 'tube' will be inserted, using the handle of the crochet hook to help.

Thread a long needle with the tail of yarn from the 'tube' and pass it up through the opening in the head, bringing it out on top *(see photo 9)*. Use this yarn to guide the head on to the tube until it reaches round 30. This will make it more stable. Knot yarn at top of head and weave in end.

Sew the head to the neck, passing the needle through the loops of the sts of the last round of the head and between the sts of the neck. Cut yarn and weave in ends.

7

8

9

10

Hair

Using Hobbii Mohair Delight yarn (KK) – 3.5mm (UK 9, US E4) crochet hook.

Note: it is also possible to crochet using Hobbii Diablo doubled or in cotton (see page 17).

Round 1: 6 dc into a MR (6 sts).
Round 2: 2 dc in each st around (12 sts).
Round 3: (1 dc, 2 dc in the next st) six times (18 sts).
Round 4: (2 dc, 2 dc in the next st) six times (24 sts).
Round 5: (3 dc, 2 dc in the next st) six times (30 sts).
Round 6: (4 dc, 2 dc in the next st) six times (36 sts).
Round 7: (5 dc, 2 dc in the next st) six times (42 sts).
Round 8: (13 dc, 2 dc in the next st) three times (45 sts).
Rounds 9–15: 1 dc in each st around (45 sts). (The number of rounds can be adapted depending on the yarn used and your own crocheting style. Try the hairpiece before you work the last round). Place a stitch marker in the last stitch.
Continue in rows.

Row 16: 24 dc (24 sts). Do not work the other sts but turn.
Row 17: 1 ch, sk 2 sts, 43 dc (ignore the stitch marker). (43 sts). Turn.
Row 18: 1 ch, sk 2 sts, 18 dc (18 sts).

Note: you should have reached the stitch marker.

Continue in rounds directly after the stitch marker.

Round 19: 15 dc, sk 1 st, 1 sl st, 5 dc, 2 dc on the edge of rows 16 and 17, 2 sl st in the parting, 1 sl st, 4 ch, 1 sl st on the edge *(see photo 10)* and continue with the short strands (4 ch, 1 sl st in the next st) six times, (3 ch, 1 sl st in the next st) twice, 8 dc. Join round with 1 sl st and leave a long tail of yarn for sewing up.

Adjust the hairpiece on the head, positioning the parting on the forehead *(see photo 11)*, then sew into place, working the yarn through the sts of the last round.

Cut yarn and weave in ends.

> ***Tip***
> ***Gently brush the hair with a little metal brush to make the fibres stand out.***

Using dark brown or black embroidery thread, embroider the eyes at round 19 (tenth round from the bottom of the head, spacing them 10 sts apart *(see photo 12)*.

Spectacles

Use yarn (AA).

Use the wire to make the spectacles, winding cotton yarn around to cover the wire *(see instructions on page 16) (see photo 13)*.

Jeans

Use yarn (P).

Round 1: work 42 ch, then join with 1 dc into first ch (counts as first st of round), ensuring that the chain is not twisted) and work 1 dc in each st around (42 sts).
Round 2: 1 dc in each st around (42 sts).
Round 3: 10 dc, 2 dc in the next st, 20 dc, 2 dc in the next st, 10 dc (44 sts).
Rounds 4–10: 1 dc in each st around (44 sts). Mark the mid-point between the legs. Allow 21 sts for each leg.

Note: 1 dc remains free between the two legs (mark with pins) *(see photo 14)**.*

Join the last st of the back to the first st of the front with 1 dc (counts as first dc of round).

The sts of first leg now form a round *(see photo 15)*.

Continue working as follows:

Rounds 11–33: 1 dc in each st around (21 sts).
Round 34: work 3 or 4 dc to reach inside of leg and move stitch marker. Then work 1 dc in flo of each st around to form the turn-up (21 sts). Finish with 1 sl st. Fasten off and sew the turn-up in place with a few stitches. Weave in ends.
Second leg: join yarn at back of work, next to pin and work 1 dc in each of next 21 sts (21 sts). Join in a round and rep rounds 12 to 34 (21 sts).
Finish with 1 sl st.

Fasten off and sew the turn-up in place with a few stitches. Weave in end.

Sew up opening between legs with a needle.

Weave in end.

11

12

13

14

15

Waistband

Use yarn (P).

Join the yarn in first st of round 1 and work 1 dc in each st around (42 sts).

Finish with 1 sl st. Cut yarn and weave in ends.

Embroider a line in backstitch between rounds 1 and 2 using the white embroidery thread for the seam.

Project continues overleaf

Belt

Use yarn (AA).
Work 44 ch. Leave a long tail of yarn so you can sew together at a later stage.

Place the waistband around the top of the trousers (with the starting and finishing tails of the waistband at the back) and sew in place with a few stitches.
Weave in ends.
Embroider the belt loops using yarn (P) over the belt *(see photo 16)*.

Blazer

Use yarn (BB).
The blazer is worked in rows, from top to bottom.

Note: the 1 ch at the end of the row does not count as a stitch; it is only used to turn the work.

Row 1: work 35 ch, then starting in the second ch from hook, 1 dc in each st around, 1 ch, turn (34 sts).
Row 2: 8 dc, 2 dc in the next st, 16 dc, 2 dc in the next st, 8 dc, 1 ch, turn (36 sts).
Row 3: 6 dc, 7 ch, sk 7 sts, 10 dc, 7 ch, sk 7 sts, 6 dc, 1 ch, turn (36 sts).
Row 4: 5 dc, 2 dc in the next st, 7 dc, 2 dc in the next st, 8 dc, 2 dc in the next st, 7 dc, 2 dc in the next st, 5 dc, 1 ch, turn (40 sts).
Row 5: 1 dc in each st around, 1 ch, turn (40 sts).
Row 6: 10 dc, 2 dc in the next st, 18 dc, 2 dc in the next st, 10 dc, 1 ch, turn (42 sts).
Rows 7–10: 1 dc in each st around, 1 ch, turn (42 sts).
Row 11: 11 dc, 2 dc in the next st, 18 dc, 2 dc in the next st, 11 dc, 1 ch, turn (44 sts).
Rows 12–15: 1 dc in each st around, 1 ch, turn (44 sts).
Row 16: 12 dc, 2 dc in the next st, 18 dc, 2 dc in the next st, 12 dc, 1 ch, turn (46 sts).
Rows 17 and 18: 1 dc in each st around, 1 ch, turn (46 sts).
Row 19: 13 dc, 2 dc in the next st, 18 dc, 2 dc in the next st, 13 dc, 1 ch, turn (48 sts).
Rows 20–23: 1 dc in each st around, 1 ch, turn (48 sts).
Row 24: 1 dc in each st around (48 sts).
1 ch, do not fasten off and work a border of 24 dc up the front of the body of the jacket (working in the spaces between the rows) *(see photo 17)*, 1 ch, 29 dc across the neckhole (do not work the remaining 5 sts). then form the neck as follows:
Row 25: 1 ch, turn, 24 dc (do not work the remaining 5 sts), 1 ch, turn (24 sts).
Row 26: 1 dc in each st across (24 sts). 1 ch then 1 dc at the base of the neck, 1 dc in the remaining 4 sts, 1 ch then 23 dc back down the opening (working in the spaces between the rows) *(see photo 18)*.
Fasten off and weave in ends.
Weave in starting thread too.

16

17

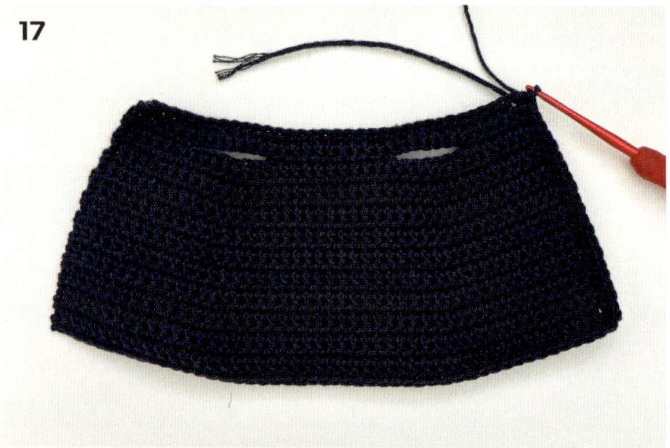

18

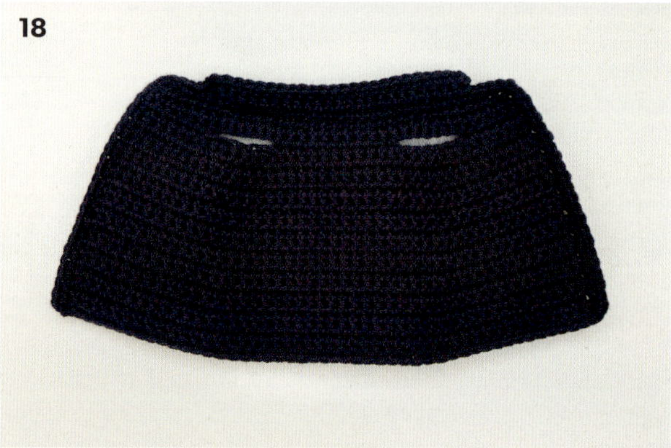

The sleeves

Use yarn (BB).
Work around the armhole space.
Join yarn with 1 ch to side of row 3 and work 7 htr around the top of the armhole, 1 htr in the st on the side, 7 dc round the bottom of the armhole, 1 htr in the st on the side (16 sts) *(see photo 19)*.
Then continue in htr for 12 rounds (16 sts).
Finish round with 1 dc and 1 sl st to even out the length.
Cut yarn and weave in ends.
Do the same for second sleeve.
If necessary, mist the blazer with water and iron to flatten out.

Basketball boot (make two)

Use yarns (E) and (BB) *(see photo 20)*.
Start with the sole using yarn (E).
Work 8 ch.

Note: sts will be crocheted on both sides of chain.

Round 1: starting in second ch from hook, 6 dc, 3 dc in first ch; continue on other side, 5 dc, 2 dc in the next st (16 sts).
Round 2: 2 dc in the next st, 5 dc, 2 dc in next 3 sts, 6 dc, 2 dc in the next st (21 sts).
Round 3: 2 dc in the next st, 8 dc, 2 dc in next 3 sts, 8 dc, 2 dc in the next st (26 sts).
Round 4: dc in blo of each st around (26 sts), changing to yarn (BB) on last yrh.
Rounds 5 and 6: 1 dc in each st around (26 sts).
Round 7: 9 dc, 4 dc2tog, 9 dc (22 sts).
Round 8: 9 dc, 2 dc2tog, 9 dc (20 sts).
Round 9: 8 dc, 2 dc2tog, 8 dc (18 sts).
Finish with 1 sl st, cut yarn and weave in ends.

Embroider a line in backstitch between rounds 4 and 5, using red embroidery thread and 3 small lines using yarn (E) on the front of the boot for the laces.

Making the accessories *(see photo 21)*

Cap

Use yarn (S).
Round 1: 6 dc into a MR (6 sts).
Round 2: 2 dc in each st around (12 sts).
Round 3: (1 dc, 2 dc in the next st) six times (18 sts).
Round 4: (2 dc, 2 dc in the next st) six times (24 sts).
Round 5: (3 dc, 2 dc in the next st) six times (30 sts).
Round 6: (4 dc, 2 dc in the next st) six times (36 sts).
Round 7: (5 dc, 2 dc in the next st) six times (42 sts).
Round 8: (6 dc, 2 dc in the next st) six times (48 sts).
Round 9: (7 dc, 2 dc in the next st) six times (54 sts).
Round 10: (8 dc, 2 dc in the next st) six times (60 sts).
Round 11: 21 dc, (2 dc in the next st, 2 dc) five times, 2 dc in the next st, 23 dc (66 sts).
Round 12: 22 dc, (2 dc in the next st, 3 dc) five times, 2 dc in the next st, 23 dc (72 sts).
Rounds 13–16: 1 dc in each st around (72 sts).
Round 17: 28 dc, (dc2tog, 6 dc) twice, dc2tog, 26 dc (69 sts).
Round 18: 25 dc, (dc2tog, 2 dc) five times, dc2tog, 22 dc (63 sts).
Round 19: 25 dc, (2 dc in blo of the next st, 2 dc in blo) five times, 2 dc in blo of the next st, 22 dc (69 sts).
Round 20: 20 dc, 5 sl st, 3 dc, 2 dc in next st, 12 htr, 2 dc in next st, 3 dc, 5 sl st, 18 dc, 1 sl st (71 sts).
Cut yarn and weave in ends *(see photo 22)*.

19

20

21

22

Project continues overleaf

Camera

Use yarns (S), (O) and (T).

Start the camera using yarn (S). Work 10 ch.

Note: sts will be crocheted on both sides of chain.

Round 1: starting in second ch from hook, 8 dc, 3 dc in first of ch-10; continue on other side. 7 dc, 2 dc in the next st (20 sts).
Rounds 2–5: 1 dc in each st around (20 sts), changing to yarn (O) on last yrh.
Rounds 6 and 7: 1 dc in each st around (20 sts). Join the round with 1 sl st and leave a long tail of yarn for sewing up (knot and cut yarn (S)).

Lens

Use yarns (T) and (O).

Start with yarn (T).

Round 1: 6 dc into a MR (6 sts).
Round 2: 2 dc in each st around (12 sts), changing to yarn (O) on last yrh.
Round 3: 1 dc in each st around (12 sts).
Join the round with 1 sl st and leave a long tail of yarn for sewing up (knot and cut yarn (T)).

Sew the lens to the front of the camera and weave in end. Sew up the opening at the top of the camera with a darning needle, passing the yarn through the blo of the sts.

Weave in end.

Handle

Use yarn (S).

Work 61 ch, then starting in the second ch from hook, work 1 sl st in each st around (60 sts).

Leave a long tail of yarn so you can sew on the strap to either side of the camera.

Weave in ends.

Dog

Use yarns (E) and (X) and a little of yarn (F).

Head

Use yarn (E).

Stuff head as you go.

Round 1: 6 dc into a MR (6 sts).
Round 2: 2 dc in each st around (12 sts).
Round 3: (1 dc, 2 dc in the next st) six times (18 sts).
Round 4: (2 dc, 2 dc in the next st) six times (24 sts).
Round 5: 1 dc in each st around (24 sts).
Round 6: (3 dc, 2 dc in the next st) six times (30 sts).
Rounds 7–11: 1 dc in each st around (30 sts).
Round 12: (1 dc, dc2tog) ten times (20 sts).
Round 13: 10 dc2tog (10 sts).

Cut a length of yarn and sew up the opening with the darning needle, passing the needle through flo of the sts of the last round to pull tight.

Weave in end.

23

Ear (make two)

Use yarn (X).

Round 1: 6 dc into a MR (6 sts).
Round 2: (1 dc, 2 dc in the next st) three times (9 sts).
Rounds 3–6: 1 dc in each st around (9 sts).
Round 7: (1 dc, dc2tog) three times (6 sts).
Pinch the edges together and sew up with 3 dc into sts on both sides at same time. Leave a long tail of yarn so you can sew them to either side of the head at round 5.

Muzzle

Use yarn (E).

Work 5 ch.

Note: sts will be crocheted on both sides of chain.

Round 1: starting in second ch from hook, 2 dc in the next st, 2 dc, 4 dc in first of ch-5; continue on the other side, 2 dc, 2 dc in the next st (12 sts).
Round 2: 1 dc in each st around (12 sts).
Cut a length of yarn to sew the muzzle to the head.

Weave in ends *(see photo 23)*.

Embroider the nose and eyes using black yarn.

Body

Use yarn (E).

Stuff head as you go.

Round 1: 7 dc into a MR (7 sts).
Round 2: 2 dc in each st around (14 sts).
Round 3: (1 dc, 2 dc in the next st) seven times (21 sts).
Round 4: (1 dc, 2 dc in the next st) three times, 9 dc, (1 dc, 2 dc in the next st) three times (27 sts).
Rounds 5–7: 1 dc in each st around (27 sts).
Round 8: 3 dc2tog, 15 dc, 3 dc2tog (21 sts).
Round 9: 2 dc2tog, 15 dc, dc2tog (18 sts).
Round 10: (1 dc, dc2tog) six times (12 sts).
Finish round with 1 sl st.

Fasten off, leaving enough yarn to sew the body under the head. At the chin, weave the yarn between the sts of the body rather than under the loops of the last round to pull the head down slightly. Fasten off and weave in end.

Tail

Use yarn (E).

Work 35 ch, then starting in the second ch from hook, work 1 dc in each st around (4 sts). Cut a length of yarn to sew the tail to the back. Fasten off and weave in end.

Front paw (make two)

Use yarn (E).

Round 1: 6 dc into a MR (6 sts).
Rounds 2–6: 1 dc in each st around (6 sts).
Pinch the edges together and sew up with 3 dc into sts on both sides at same time.

Leave a long tail of yarn to sew them to the front of body, at a slight angle.

Add a stitch under the paws to keep them pointing forwards.

Back leg (make two)

Use yarn (E).

Round 1: 6 dc into a MR (6 sts).
Round 2: 2 dc, 2 dc in the next st, 3 dc (7 sts).
Rounds 3 and 4: 1 dc in each st around (7 sts).
Pinch the edges together and sew up with 3 dc into sts on both sides at same time.

Leave a long tail of yarn to sew them to each side of the body, at a slight angle *(see photo 24)*.

Collar

Use yarn (F).

Work 18 ch and knot around the neck, then weave the ends into the body *(see photo 25)*. Make a lead with a length of yarn of the same colour.

24

25

The Sisters

At the ripe old age of 12, Lola takes her role of big sister to heart, while at the same time affirming her independence. She loves organizing craft sessions for her brother and sisters as well as spending hours alone at the skate park with her headphones on, combining her two loves of skateboarding and pop music.

Susan is about to celebrate her fourth birthday and can't wait to decorate the cake and get the house ready with her brother and sisters and, of course, to unwrap her presents! Especially since Grandma and Grandpa will be joining the party!

Lola

THE BIG SISTER

Finished height: 24cm (9½in)

You will need

DMC Natura Just Cotton (4-ply/fingering) yarn, 50g/1¾oz/155m/170yd, in (R), (Y), (I), (S) and (A) and a little of yarns (L) and (H)

DMC Merino Essentiel 3 (4-ply/fingering) merino blend, 50g/1¾oz/200m/218yd for some of the clothes, in (CC) and (DD)

Hobbii Diablo (1–3-ply/lace weight) yarn, 50g/1¾oz/225m/246yd, in (FF), for the hair (it is also possible to use DMC Natura Just Cotton – see page 17)

Dark brown (or black) and red embroidery thread

2.25mm (UK 13, US B1) crochet hook, 3mm (UK 11, US 2/3) crochet hook for the hair

4 small buttons and a piece of stiff cardboard

Stiff wire

Basic tools and materials (see pages 10–12)

Special stitches:

3-treble bobble (3 tr for thumbs), raised front-post half-treble, raised back-post half-treble

Making the doll

Note: unless stated otherwise, always work in spiral rounds using a 2.25mm (UK 13, US B1) crochet hook.

Body

Note: start with the legs.

Leg (make two)

Use yarn (O). Stuff legs as you go.

Work 5 ch.

Note: sts will be crocheted on both sides of chain.

Round 1: starting in second ch from hook, 3 dc, 3 dc in last of 5-ch; continue on other side. 2 dc, 2 dc in the next st (10 sts).
Round 2: 2 dc in the next st, 2 dc, 2 dc in next 3 sts, 3 dc, 2 dc in the next st (15 sts).
Round 3: 1 dc in each st around (15 sts).
Round 4: 5 dc, 3 dc2tog, 4 dc (12 sts).
Round 5: 4 dc, 2 dc2tog, 4 dc (10 sts).
Rounds 6–25: 1 dc in each st around (10 sts).
Round 26: 2 dc, 2 dc in the next st, 4 dc, 2 dc in the next st, 2 dc (12 sts).
Rounds 27–30: 1 dc in each st around (12 sts).
Round 31: work 9 dc to reach the side. Finish with 1 sl st.
Fasten off and weave in end.
Finish stuffing.

Crochet the second leg in same way as far as round 30.
Round 31: 1 dc in each st around (12 sts). Work another 4 dc to reach inside of leg *(see photo 1)*.
Do not cut the yarn but continue as follows:

Body

Use yarns (O), (R) and (A).
Stuff body as you go.
Lay the two legs side by side, toes up and after second leg, 4 ch and join to first leg with 1 dc (counts as first dc of round).
Round 1: 1 dc in each of 12 sts around first leg, 1 dc in 4 sts of chain, 12 dc in each of 12 sts of the other leg and 1 dc in 4 sts on other side of chain (12 + 4 + 12 + 4 = 32 sts) *(see photo 2)*. Place stitch marker here (it will be on doll's front).
Rounds 2–7: 1 dc in each st around (32 sts).
Round 8: 23 dc to reach left side, changing to yarn (R) on last yrh (23 sts).
Move stitch marker.
Round 9: (blo), 1 dc in each st around (32 sts).
Rounds 10–12: 1 dc in each st around (32 sts).
Round 13: (6 dc, dc2tog) four times (28 sts).
Rounds 14 and 15: 1 dc in each st around (28 sts).
Round 16: (5 dc, dc2tog) four times (24 sts).
Rounds 17 and 18: 1 dc in each st around (24 sts).
Round 19: (4 dc, dc2tog) four times (20 sts).
Round 20: 1 dc in each st around (20 sts).

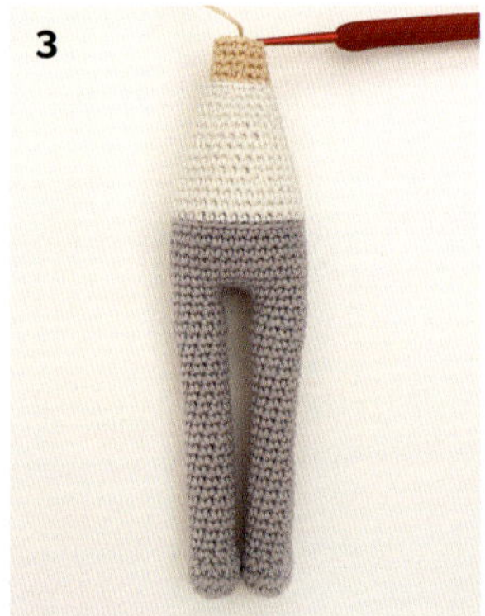

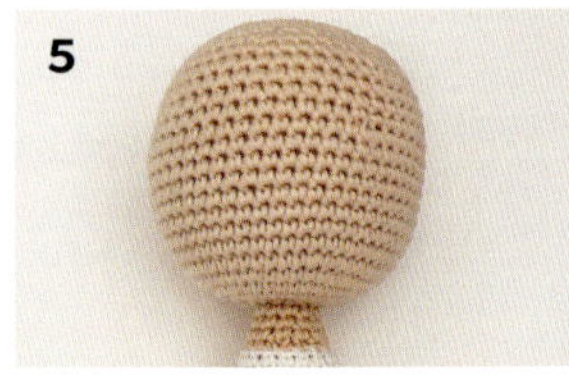

Round 21: (3 dc, dc2tog) four times (16 sts), changing to yarn (A) on last yrh.
Round 22: (blo), 1 dc in each st around (16 sts).
Round 23: (2 dc, dc2tog) four times (12 sts).
Rounds 24 and 25: 1 dc in each st around (12 sts) *(see photo 3)*. Finish stuffing. Do not cut yarn but continue directly with head.

Head

Use yarn (A).
Stuff head as you go.
Round 1: 2 dc in each st around (24 sts).
Round 2: (1 dc, 2 dc in the next st) twelve times (36 sts).
Round 3: (5 dc, 2 dc in the next st) six times (42 sts).
Round 4: 3 dc, 2 dc in the next st, (6 dc, 2 dc in the next st) five times, 3 dc (48 sts).
Round 5: (15 dc, 2 dc in the next st) three times (51 sts).

Note: to make the neck more stable, slip a pipe cleaner (chenille stick) into the opening *(see photo 4)*.

Rounds 6–13: 1 dc in each st around (51 sts).
Round 14: (15 dc, dc2tog) three times (48 sts).
Rounds 15–18: 1 dc in each st around (48 sts).
Round 19: (6 dc, dc2tog) six times (42 sts).
Round 20: (5 dc, dc2tog) six times (36 sts).
Round 21: (4 dc, dc2tog) six times (30 sts).
Round 22: (3 dc, dc2tog) six times (24 sts).

Round 23: (2 dc, dc2tog) six times (18 sts).
Round 24: (1 dc, dc2tog) six times (12 sts).
Round 25: 6 dc2tog (6 sts).
Cut a length of yarn. Finish stuffing. Sew up the opening with the darning needle, passing the needle through flo of the sts of the last round to pull tight. Weave in end *(see photo 5)*.

Arms

Crocheted separately using yarns (A) and (R).

Start with yarn (A).

Round 1: 6 dc into a MR (6 sts).
Round 2: (2 dc, 2 dc in the next st) twice (8 sts).
Round 3: 1 dc in each st around (8 sts).
Round 4: 3 dc, 1 bobble st (thumb), 4 dc (8 sts).
Round 5: 1 dc in each st around (8 sts).
Round 6: 2 dc, dc2tog, 4 dc (7 sts).
Round 7: 1 dc in each st around (7 sts). Stuff hand lightly (using a wooden skewer or crochet hook handle to help).
Continue, using yarn (R).

Rounds 8–22: 1 dc in each st around (7 sts).
Pinch top of arm together, ensuring that the thumb points to the side of the body (add or sk 1 dc if necessary) and sew up with 3 dc into sts on both sides at same time. Cut, leaving sufficient yarn for making up.

Sew the arms on either side of the body, at round 21, ensuring the thumbs are facing in the right direction *(see photo 6)*.

Hair

Use Hobbii Diablo yarn (FF) – crochet hook 3mm (UK 11, US 2/3).

Note: it is also possible to use cotton yarn (see page 17).

Hairpiece

Round 1: 6 dc into a MR (6 sts).
Round 2: 2 dc in each st around (12 sts).
Round 3: (1 dc, 2 dc in the next st) six times (18 sts).
Round 4: (2 dc, 2 dc in the next st) six times (24 sts).
Round 5: (3 dc, 2 dc in the next st) six times (30 sts).
Round 6: (4 dc, 2 dc in the next st) six times (36 sts).
Round 7: (5 dc, 2 dc in the next st) six times (42 sts).
Round 8: (6 dc, 2 dc in the next st) six times (48 sts).
Round 9: (15 dc, 2 dc in the next st) three times (51 sts).
Rounds 10–23: 1 dc in each st around (51 sts).

6

7

8

9

(The number of rounds can be adapted depending on the yarn used and your own crocheting style. Try the hairpiece before you work the last round).
Round 24: 6 dc, dc2tog, 6 htr, 10 tr, sk 1 st, 1 sl st, sk 1 st, 10 tr, 6 htr, dc2tog, 6 dc (47 sts).
Finish the work with 1 sl st, leaving a long tail of yarn for sewing up.
Adjust the hairpiece on the head, positioning the sl st in the middle of the forehead *(see photo 7)* and holding in place with pins.

Braids

Cut 18 strands, each 20cm (8in) in length (9 strands for each braid).
Mark the position of the braids on either side of the hairpiece. Using the crochet hook, pull the lengths through the st of the last round and fold in half *(see photo 8)*. Secure 4 long strands on the forehead which will be taken into the braids and 4 shorter ones for the fringe *(see photo 9)*.
Plait the braids taking two long strands of the fringe into each one and tying them at the ends with a length of yarn. Trim the ends evenly with a pair of scissors. Sew the hairpiece on to the head, following the sts of the last round. Cut and weave in ends.

Project continues overleaf

> *Tip*
> ***Gently brush the hair with a little metal brush to make the fibres stand out.***

Embroider the eyes in dark brown or black embroidery thread at round 9, spaced 9 sts apart.

For a healthy glow, add a little colour to the cheeks using a piece of cloth rubbed with a red crayon *(see photo 10)*.

Shorts

Use yarn (Y).

Round 1: work 36 ch, then join with 1 dc into first ch (counts as first st of round), ensuring that the chain is not twisted) and work 1 dc in each st around (36 sts).

Rounds 2–10: 1 dc in each st around (36 sts). Mark the mid-point between the legs. Allow 17 sts for each leg.

Note: 1 dc remains free on either side between the two legs (mark with pins) *(see photo 11).*

Join the last st of the back to the first st of the front with 1 dc (counts as first dc of round).

The sts of first leg now form a round *(see photo 12)*.

Continue working as follows:

Round 11: 1 dc in each st around (17 sts).

Round 12: 1 sl st in each st around (17 sts).

Cut yarn and weave in ends.

Second leg: join yarn at back of work, next to pin and work 1 dc in each of next 17 sts (17 sts). Join round and work 1 sl st in each st around (17 sts). Cut yarn and weave in ends.

Sew up opening between legs with a needle. Weave in ends. Weave in starting thread too.

Garment variation: use the colour of your choice. To make full-length legs, work 18 additional rounds after round 11. Cut yarn and weave in ends.

Sweater

Use DMC Merino Essentiel 3 yarn (DD) and a little of yarn (Y).

Note: it is also possible to use cotton yarn.

The sweater is worked in rows.

Note: the 1 ch at the end of the row does not count as a stitch; it is only used to turn the work.

Row 1: work 25 ch, then starting in the second ch from hook, 1 dc in each st across, 1 ch, turn (24 sts).

Row 2: (4 dc, 2 dc in the next st) twice, 4 dc, (2 dc in the next st, 4 dc) twice, 1 ch, turn (28 sts).

Row 3: 2 dc in the next st, 9 dc, 2 dc in the next st, 6 dc, 2 dc in the next st, 9 dc, 2 dc in the next st, 1 ch, turn (32 sts).

Row 4: 4 dc, 6 ch, sk 7 sts, 10 dc, 6 ch, sk 7 sts, 4 dc, 1 ch, turn (30 sts).

Row 5: 10 dc, 2 dc in the next st, 8 dc, 2 dc in the next st, 10 dc, 1 ch, turn (32 sts).

Row 6: 10 dc, 2 dc in the next st, 10 dc, 2 dc in the next st, 10 dc, 1 ch, turn (34 sts).

10

11

12

13

14

15

Row 7: 8 dc, 2 dc in the next st, 16 dc, 2 dc in the next st, 8 dc, 1 ch, turn (36 sts).
Row 8: (5 dc, 2 dc in the next st) twice, 12 dc, (2 dc in the next st, 5 dc) twice, 1 ch, turn (40 sts).
Row 9: 1 dc in each st across, 1 ch, turn (40 sts) *(see photo 13)*.
Row 10: 14 dc, 2 dc in the next st, 10 dc, 2 dc in the next st, 14 dc, 1 ch, turn (42 sts).
Rows 11 and 12: 1 dc in each st around, 1 ch, turn (42 sts).
Row 13: 8 dc, 2 dc in the next st, 24 dc, 2 dc in the next st, 8 dc, 1 ch, turn (44 sts).
Rows 14 to 19: 1 dc in each st across, 1 ch, turn (44 sts).
Do not cut yarn and continue to work the ribbing, alternating front-post htr and back post htr. *(See pages 21–22. If you are not confident working this stitch, just crochet an additional row of dc.)*

Namely, 1 ch then: yrh, insert the hook (from front to back). around the post of the st of the previous row (just under the loops), yrh and draw it back out to the front and complete the htr. Yrh again, insert the hook in the back of the work, from back from front, around the post of the next st and complete the htr. Continue in the same way to the end of the row *(see photo 14)*.

Leave a long tail of yarn for sewing up.

Sleeves

Use DMC Merino Essentiel 3 yarn (DD).

Work around the armhole space.

Join yarn to side of row 4 and work 7 dc around the top of the armhole, 1 dc in the st on the side, 6 dc round the bottom of the armhole, 1 dc in the st on the side (15 sts).

Then work 15 htr for 8 rounds and 15 dc in blo (15 sts). Finish round with 1 dc and 1 sl st to even out the length.

Cut yarn and weave in all ends invisibly.

Rep for the second sleeve *(see photo 15)*.

Using yarn (Y), crochet a border of dc around round 1 (in the chain) of the neckhole.

Leave a long tail of yarn at the start and end so you can knot the opening.

Note: it is also possible to sew on a button and make a button loop.

Sew up the opening in the back to around row 10.

Embroider a star using yarn (Y) on the front of the sweater and a line in backstitch around row 19 *(see photo 16)*.

Basketball boot (make two)

Use yarns (I) and (R) and a little red embroidery thread.

Start with the sole using yarn (I). Work 6 ch.

Note: sts will be crocheted on both sides of chain.

Round 1: starting in second ch from hook, 4 dc, 3 dc in first ch; continue on other side, 3 dc, 2 dc in the next st (12 sts).
Round 2: 2 dc in the next st, 3 dc, 2 dc in each of the next 3 sts, 4 dc, 2 dc in the next st (17 sts).

16

17

Round 3: 2 dc in the next 2 sts, 4 dc, 2 dc in the next 4 sts, 5 dc, 2 dc in the next st, 1 dc (24 sts).
Round 4: 1 dc in blo of each st around (24 sts), changing to yarn (R) on last yrh.
Rounds 5 and 6: 1 dc in each st around (24 sts).
Round 7: 9 dc, 4 dc2tog, 7 dc (20 sts).
Round 8: 7 dc, 4 dc2tog, 5 dc (16 sts).
Round 9: 1 sl st in each st around (16 sts).
Finish with 1 sl st, cut yarn and weave in ends.

Embroider a line in backstitch between rounds 4 and 5 using the red embroidery thread and 2 small dashes using yarn (I) on the front of the basket for the laces *(see photo 17)*.

Leg warmers (make two)

Using DMC Merino Essentiel 3 yarn (CC).

Round 1: work 14 ch, then join with 1 dc into first ch (counts as first st of round), ensuring that the chain is not twisted) and work 1 dc in each st around (14 sts).
Rounds 2–8: 1 dc in each st around (14 sts).
Finish round with 1 sl st.

Cut yarn and weave in ends. Weave in starting thread too.

Project continues overleaf

Making the accessories

Headphones

Use yarns (R) and (O).

Headband

Use yarn (R) and a 30cm (12in) length of stiff wire.

Note: worked in rows.

Row 1: work 37 ch, then starting in second ch from hook, 1 dc in each ch across (36 sts).
Rows 2 and 3: 1 ch, turn, 1 dc in each st around (26 sts).
Fasten off to secure, leaving enough yarn for making up.

Make two circles with a diameter of approximately 2cm (¾in). at each end of the piece of wire and bend into the shape of headphones.
Check the size on the doll's head and adjust as required.

Inside (make two)

Use yarn (O).
Round 1: 6 dc into a MR (6 sts).
Round 2: 2 dc in each st around (12 sts).
Round 3: (1 dc, 2 dc in the next st) six times (18 sts).
Round 4: (2 dc, 2 dc in the next st) six times (24 sts).
Join with 1 sl st. Cut yarn and weave in end.

Outside (make two)

Use yarn (R).
Round 1: 6 dc into a MR (6 sts).
Round 2: 2 dc in each st around (12 sts).
Round 3: (1 dc, 2 dc in the next st) six times (18 sts).
Round 4: (2 dc, 2 dc in the next st) six times (24 sts).
Round 5: 1 dc in blo of each st around (24 sts). Do not cut yarn but continue making up as follows *(see photo 18)*:
Place the white circle on the metal ring, face down, then the (O) circle on top of it, wrong sides together. Work 1 dc in each st around, inserting the hook through both the sts of the outside circle and flo of the sts of the inside circle. Cut yarn and weave in ends.
Sew the covering of the headband around the wire then to the top of the earphone.
Rep for the second earpad. Weave in ends *(see photo 19)*.

Embroider a line in backstitch around round 5 on the outside of the earphone using red embroidery thread *(see photo 20)*.

Skateboard

Use yarns (L), (Y) and (S), a short strip of cardboard and four buttons. You will crochet two board shapes, which will then be sewn together.

18

19

20

21

22

Board 1

Use yarn (L).
Work 19 ch.

Note: sts will be crocheted on both sides of chain.

Round 1: starting in second ch from hook, 2 dc in the next st, 16 dc, 4 dc in first ch; continue on other side. 16 dc, 2 dc in the next st (40 sts), changing to yarn (Y) on last yrh.
Round 2: 2 dc in the next 2 sts, 16 dc, 2 dc in the next 4 sts, 16 dc, 2 dc in the next 2 sts (48 sts).
Round 3: 2 dc in the next 4 sts, 16 dc, 2 dc in next 8 sts, 16 dc, 2 dc in the next 3 sts, 1 dc (63 sts). Finish the round with 1 sl st.
Cut yarn and weave in ends.
Cut a piece of cardboard the size of the board.

Board 2

Use yarn (S).
Work 19 ch.

Note: sts will be crocheted on both sides of chain.

Round 1: starting in second ch from hook, 2 dc in the next st, 16 dc, 4 dc in first ch; continue on other side: 16 dc, 2 dc in the next st (40 sts).
Round 2: 2 dc in the next 2 sts, 16 dc, 2 dc in the next 4 sts, 16 dc, 2 dc in the next 2 sts (48 sts).
Round 3: 2 dc in the next 4 sts, 16 dc, 2 dc in next 8 sts, 16 dc, 2 dc in the next 3 sts, 1 dc (63 sts) *(see photo 21)*.
Do not cut yarn.

Position the boards on top of each other, with wrong sides together and working in blo of the stitches opposite each other: 4 dc, 2 dc in the next 2 sts (should be on the side of the curved edge), 22 dc, 2 dc in the next 2 sts, 6 dc, 2 dc in the next 2 sts (insert the cardboard between the two layers, 22 dc, 2 dc in the next 2 sts, 1 dc (71 sts). Join with 1 sl st. Cut yarn and weave in ends *(see photo 22)*.

Axle (make two)

Use yarn (S) and four buttons.

Note: worked in rows.

Note: the 1 ch at the end of the row does not count as a stitch; it is only used to turn the work.

Row 1: work 7 ch, starting in second ch from hook, 1 dc in each st to end, 1 ch, turn (6 sts).
Rows 2–4: 1 dc in each st to end, 1 ch, turn (6 sts).
Row 5: 1 dc in each st to end (6 sts). Leave a long tail of yarn for sewing up.
Roll the axle into a tube and use a few sts to sew up.
Then sew it on to the back of the board.
Sew a button on either end of the axle *(see photo 23)*.
Rep for the second axle.
Cut yarn and weave in ends.

Drawstring bag

Use yarns (H), (I) and (R).

Note: always change yarn colour on the last yrh of the round in question. Leave the unused yarn hanging on the wrong side of the work, continue with the new colour, then pick up the waiting yarn at the stated round.

Start with yarn (H).
Round 1: 6 dc into a MR (6 sts).
Round 2: 2 dc in each st around (12 sts).
Round 3: (1 dc, 2 dc in the next st) six times (18 sts).
Round 4: (2 dc, 2 dc in the next st) six times (24 sts).
Round 5: (3 dc, 2 dc in the next st) six times (30 sts).
Round 6: (4 dc, 2 dc in the next st) six times (36 sts).
Round 7: 1 dc in blo of each st around (36 sts).
Rounds 8 and 9: 1 dc in each st around (36 sts), changing to yarn (I) on last yrh.
Round 10: 1 dc in each st around (36 sts). Pick up yarn (H) again.
Round 11: 1 dc in each st around (36 sts). Pick up yarn (I) again.
Rounds 12–16: 1 dc in each st around (36 sts), changing to yarn (R) on last yrh.
Round 17: 1 dc in each st around (36 sts). Pick up yarn (I) again.
Round 18: 1 dc in each st around (36 sts). Pick up yarn (R) again.
Rounds 19–21: 1 dc in each st around (36 sts).
Round 22: (1 sl st, 2 ch) in first st, (sk 1 st, 1 htr, 1 ch) seventeen times, sk 1 st and close with 1 sl st in second of 2 ch.
Cut yarn and weave in ends *(see photo 24)*.

23

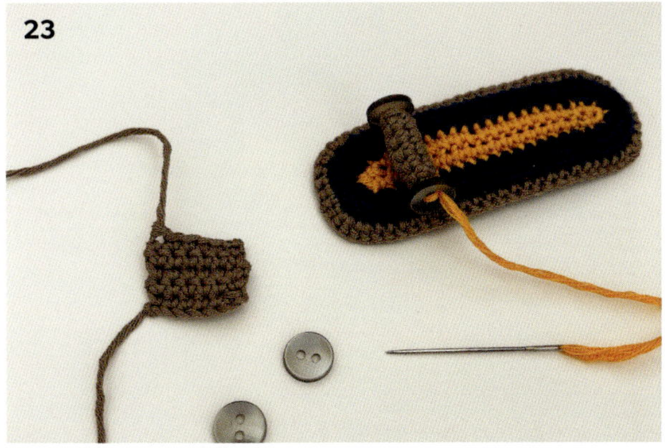

24

25

Drawstring

Use yarn (I).
Leave a 20cm (8in) tail of yarn at the start and work 100 ch (100 sts).
Fasten off, leaving enough yarn for making up.

Toggle

Use yarn (H).
Work 5 ch, then starting in second ch from hook, 4 dc (4 sts).
Cut yarn and fasten off to secure.
Fold the toggle in half and sew the ends together to form a ring.
Cut yarn and weave in ends.

Pass the drawstring through the loops of the bag, then slip the two ends through the toggle, before sewing them to the bottom to make the straps *(see photo 25)*.

Susan

THE LITTLE SISTER

Finished height: 15cm (6in)

You will need

DMC Natura Just Cotton (4-ply/fingering) yarn, 50g/1¾oz/155m/170yd, in (R), (V), (A) and (O) and a little of yarns (Z), (F), (AA), (X), (J), (C), (L) and (G)
Hobbii Diablo (1–3-ply/lace weight) yarn, 50g/1¾oz/225m/246yd, in (GG), for the hair (it is also possible to use DMC Natura Just Cotton – see page 17)
Dark brown (or black) embroidery thread
2.25mm (UK 13, US B1) crochet hook, 3mm (UK 11, US 2/3) crochet hook only for the hair
A piece of fairly stiff cardboard
Basic tools and materials (see pages 10–12)

Making the doll

Note: unless stated otherwise, always work in spiral rounds using a 2.25mm (UK 13, US B1) crochet hook.

Body

Note: start with the legs.

Leg (make two)

Use yarns (R), (A) and (V). Stuff legs as you go. Start with yarn (R).
Round 1: 5 dc into a MR (5 sts).
Round 2: 2 dc in each st around (10 sts).
Round 3: 1 dc in each st around (10 sts).
Round 4: 3 dc, 2 dc2tog, 3 dc (8 sts).
Rounds 5–8: 1 dc in each st around (8 sts), changing to yarn (A) on last yrh. Leave a 30cm (12in) tail of yarn so you can crochet the edging on the little socks at a later stage. Leave yarn (R) waiting on the outside of the work.
Round 9: 1 dc in blo of each st around (8 sts).
Rounds 10–19: 1 dc in each st around (8 sts); work an additional 3 or 4 dc to reach the back of the leg.
Finish with 1 sl st. Fasten off and weave in ends.
Finish stuffing.

Crochet the second leg in the same way to round 19. Work another 2 dc to reach inside of leg *(photo 1)* and change to yarn (V) on last yrh. Continue as follows:

Body

Use yarns (V) and (A).
Stuff body as you go. Lay the two legs side by side, toes up and after second leg, 4 ch and join to first leg with 1 dc (counts as first dc of round).
Round 1: 1 dc in each of 8 sts of first leg, 1 dc in 4 sts of chain, 1 dc in each of 8 sts of second leg and 1 dc in 4 sts on other side of chain (8 + 4 + 8 + 4 = 24 sts) *(see photo 2)*.
Place stitch marker here (it will be on doll's front).
Rounds 2–8: 1 dc in each st around (24 sts).
Round 9: (4 dc, dc2tog) four times (20 sts).
Round 10: 1 dc in each st around (20 sts).
Round 11: (3 dc, dc2tog) four times (16 sts).
Round 12: 1 dc in each st around (16 sts).
Round 13: (2 dc, dc2tog) four times (12 sts).
Round 14: work 9 dc to reach left side, changing to yarn (A) on last yrh and move stitch marker.
Round 15: 1 dc in blo of each st around (12 sts).
Rounds 16 and 17: 1 dc in each st around (12 sts).
Finish stuffing the body.
Do not cut yarn but continue directly with head *(see photo 3)*.

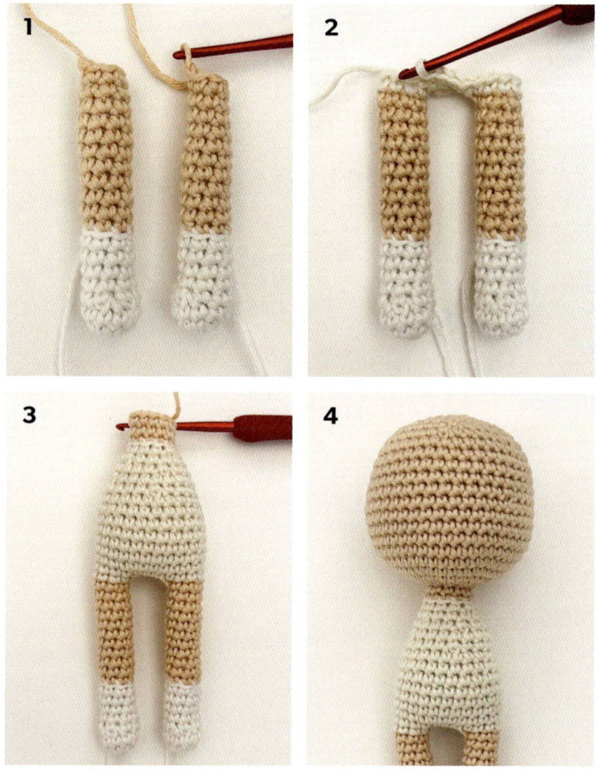

Head

Use yarn (A).
Stuff head as you go.
Round 1: 2 dc in each st around (24 sts).
Round 2: (1 dc, 2 dc in the next st) twelve times (36 sts).
Round 3: (5 dc, 2 dc in the next st) six times (42 sts).
Round 4: (13 dc, 2 dc in the next st) three times (45 sts).
Rounds 5–9: 1 dc in each st around (45 sts).
Round 10: (13 dc, dc2tog) three times (42 sts).
Rounds 11–14: 1 dc in each st around (42 sts).
Round 15: (5 dc, dc2tog) six times (36 sts).
Round 16: (4 dc, dc2tog) six times (30 sts).
Round 17: (3 dc, dc2tog) six times (24 sts).
Round 18: (2 dc, dc2tog) six times (18 sts).
Round 19: (1 dc, dc2tog) six times (12 sts).
Round 20: 6 dc2tog (6 sts).
Cut, leaving a length of yarn.
Finish stuffing, then sew up the opening with the darning needle, passing the yarn through flo of the sts of the last round to pull tight. Weave in end *(see photo 4)*.

Arm (make two)

Crocheted separately using yarns (A) and (V).
Start with yarn (A).
Round 1: 6 dc into a MR (6 sts).
Rounds 2 and 3: 1 dc in each st around (6 sts).
Round 4: 4 dc, dc2tog (5 sts).
Round 5: 1 dc in each st around (5 sts). Stuff hand lightly (using a wooden skewer or crochet hook handle to help).
Continue using yarn (V).
Rounds 6–14: 1 dc in each st around (5 sts). Pinch top of arm together and sew up with 2 dc into sts on both sides at same time.
Cut, leaving sufficient yarn for making up.

Sew the arms on either side of the body, at round 14 *(see photo 5)*.

Edging of socks

Use yarn (R) and working into flo of the sts of round 9: (1 dc in first st, 1 sl st in the next) four times, holding the doll with feet uppermost. Cut yarn and weave in ends.

Hair

Use Hobbii Diablo yarn (GG) – 3mm (UK 11, US 2/3) crochet hook.

Note: it is also possible to use cotton yarn (see page 17).

Hairpiece

Round 1: 6 dc into a MR (6 sts).
Round 2: 2 dc in each st around (12 sts).
Round 3: (1 dc, 2 dc in the next st) six times (18 sts).
Round 4: (2 dc, 2 dc in the next st) six times (24 sts).
Round 5: (3 dc, 2 dc in the next st) six times (30 sts).
Round 6: (4 dc, 2 dc in the next st) six times (36 sts).
Round 7: (5 dc, 2 dc in the next st) six times (42 sts).
Rounds 8–11: 1 dc in each st around (42 sts).
Round 12: (13 dc, 2 dc in the next st) three times (45 sts).
Rounds 13–19: 1 dc in each st around (45 sts). (The number of rounds can be adapted depending on the yarn used and your own crocheting style. Try the hairpiece before you work the last round.)
Round 20: 6 dc, dc2tog, 6 htr, 7 tr, sk 1 st, 1 sl st, sk 1 st, 7 tr, 6 htr, dc2tog, 6 dc (41 sts).
Finish the work with 1 sl st, leaving a long tail of yarn for sewing up.
Adjust the hairpiece on the head, positioning the sl st in the middle of the forehead *(see photo 6)*. Hold in place with pins.

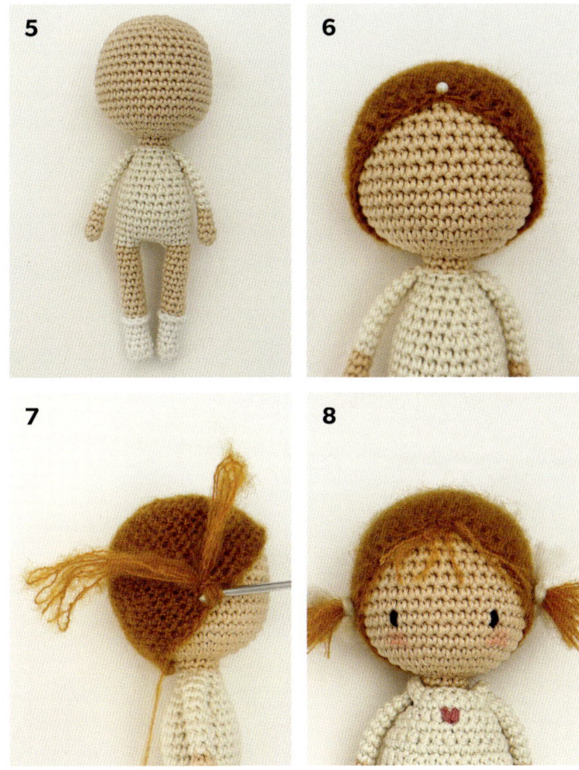

Hair bunches (make two)

Cut 24 strands, each 10cm (4in) in length (12 strands for each braid). Mark the position of the bunches on either side of the hairpiece. Using the crochet hook, pull the lengths through the relevant st of the last round and fold in half *(see photo 7)*.
Tie a strand of identical or contrasting thread around the base of the bunch.
Sew the hairpiece to the head, following the contours of the last round. Add a few stitches around the bunches to hold them in place. Cut yarn and weave in end.
Trim the ends evenly with a pair of scissors.
Tie a few strands to the forehead.

> ***Tip***
> ***Gently brush the hair with a little metal brush to make the fibres stand out.***

Embroider the eyes in dark brown (or black) embroidery thread at round 7, spaced 8 sts apart *(see photo 8)*. For a healthy glow, add a little colour to the cheeks using a piece of cloth rubbed with a red crayon.

Project continues overleaf

Romper suit

Use yarn (V).

Worked first in rows, then in rounds.

Note: the 1 ch at the end of the row does not count as a stitch; it is only used to turn the work.

Row 1: work 21 ch, then starting in the second ch from hook, 1 dc in each st across, 1 ch, turn (20 sts).
Row 2: 1 dc, 2 dc in the next st, 1 dc, 4 ch, sk 4 sts, 2 dc in the next st, 4 dc, 2 dc in the next st, 4 ch, sk 4 sts, 1 dc, 2 dc in the next st, 1 dc, 1 ch, turn (24 sts).
Row 3: 3 dc, 2 dc in the next st, 4 dc, 2 dc in the next st, 6 dc, 2 dc in the next st, 4 dc, 2 dc in the next st, 3 dc, 1 ch, turn (28 sts).
Rows 4 and 5: 1 dc in each st across, 1 ch, turn (28 sts).
Row 6: (3 dc, 2 dc in the next st) seven times, 1 ch, turn (35 sts).
Row 7: 1 dc in each st across (35 sts).
Round 8: join the 2 ends with 1 sl st, then 1 ch and continue in the round: 1 htr in each st around (35 sts).
Rounds 9–13: 1 htr in each st around (without working a ch at the start of the rounds) (35 sts).
Mark the mid-point between the legs. Allow 17 sts for each leg (possibly work 1 or 2 additional htr to reach mid-point between legs).

Note: 1 dc remains free at the front of the romper suit (mark with pins) *(see photo 9).*

Join the last st of the back to the first st of the front with 1 dc (counts as first dc of round).

The sts of the first leg now form a round *(see photo 10)*.
Continue working as follows:
Round 14: 6 dc, 3 dc2tog, 5 dc (14 sts).
Finish with 1 sl st. Fasten off and weave in end.

Second leg: join yarn at back of work, next to pin and work 5 dc, 3 dc2tog, 6 dc (14 sts). Join in a round with 1 sl st into starting ch. Cut yarn and weave in end. Sew up opening between legs with a needle.
Join two short pieces of yarn to the top corners of the back so it can be tied together.

Note: it is also possible to sew on a button and make a button loop.

Embroider a little heart on the front of the romper suit using yarn (J).

Garment variation: use the colour of your choice. To make a dress, crochet from row 1 to round 13 of the romper suit then:

Round 14: rep 1 sl st, 2 dc in the next st all around to make a pretty frill. Join with 1 sl st. Fasten off and weave in end. Join two short pieces of yarn to the top corners of the back so it can be tied together.

Note: it is also possible to sew on a button and make a button loop.

Embroider a little heart on the front of the dress using yarn (J) *(see photo 11)*.

9

10

11

Shoe (make two)

Use yarns (AA) and (J) *(see photo 12)*.
Start with the sole using yarn (AA).
Round 1: 6 dc into a MR (6 sts).
Round 2: 2 dc in each st around (12 sts).
Round 3: 2 dc in the next sts, 4 dc, 2 dc in next 3 sts, 3 dc, 2 dc in the next st (17 sts).
Round 4: 1 dc in blo of each st around (17 sts), changing to yarn (J) on last yrh.
Rounds 5 and 6: 1 dc in each st around (17 sts).
Round 7: 6 dc, 4 dc2tog, 3 dc (13 sts).
Round 8: 5 dc, 5 ch, sk 5 sts, 3 dc (13 sts).
Finish with 1 sl st. Fasten off and weave in ends.

Making the accessories

Mouse headband

Use yarn (O) and a little of yarn (J) *(see photos 13 and 14)*.

Ear (make two)

Use yarn (O). Do not stuff.
Round 1: 6 dc into a MR (6 sts).
Round 2: 2 dc in each st around (12 sts).
Round 3: (1 dc, 2 dc in the next st) six times (18 sts).
Rounds 4–7: 1 dc in each st around (18 sts).
Round 8: (1 dc, dc2tog) six times (12 sts).
Round 9: 6 dc2tog (6 sts).
Leave a long tail of yarn for sewing up. Flatten the circle to shape the ear. Make a second ear in the same way.

Headband

Use yarn (O).

Note: worked in rows.

Row 1: leave a 20cm (8in) tail of yarn at the start and work 49 ch (adapt according to the size of the doll). Start in second ch from hook and work 1 dc in each st around, 1 ch, turn (48 sts).
Row 2: 1 dc in each st around (48 sts).
Cut yarn, leaving a 20cm (8in) tail so you can knot the headband at the nape of the neck. Thread the yarn through the loop and draw tight to secure. Use a darning needle to thread the starting yarn through the end of row 1 and fasten off.

Sew the ears to the headband, spaced 10 sts apart, with a few stitches over 3 or 4 adjacent sts.

Weave in ends.

Bow

Use yarn (J).

(See 'Bow' chart, right.)

Work 9 ch.

Note: sts will be crocheted on both sides of chain.

Round 1: starting in third ch from hook: 2 htr in the first st, 2 htr, 1 sl st, 2 htr, 4 htr in first ch; continue on the other side: 2 htr, 1 sl st, 2 htr, 2 htr in the last st (18 sts). Finish the work with 1 sl st into the next st.
Cut, leaving a length of yarn; weave it in under several sts, then wrap it round the centre of the bow before sewing it to the base of the ear. Weave in ends.

12

13

14

Bow

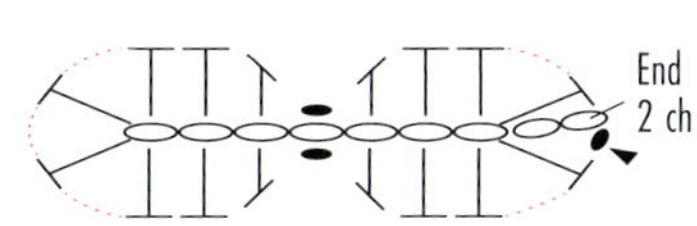

◄ Cut yarn.
⚬ **Chain stitch:** yrh, draw yarn through loop on hook.
- **Slip stitch:** insert hook through first st, yrh and draw through st and loop on hook.
T **Half-treble:** yrh, insert hook through first st, yrh and draw through st, yrh and draw through all loops on hook.

Project continues overleaf

Mouse cuddly toy

Use yarns (O) and (R) *(see photo 15)*.

Head

Use yarn (O).
Stuff head as you go.
Round 1: 6 dc into a MR (6 sts).
Round 2: 2 dc in each st around (12 sts).
Round 3: (2 dc, 2 dc in the next st) four times (16 sts).
Round 4: 1 dc in each st around (16 sts).
Round 5: (3 dc, 2 dc in the next st) four times (20 sts).
Rounds 6 and 7: 1 dc in each st around (20 sts).
Round 8: (3 dc, dc2tog) four times (16 sts).
Round 9: 8 dc2tog (8 sts).
Finish the work with 1 sl st and fasten off, leaving a long tail for making up.

Comforter

Use yarn (O).
Worked in rows.

Note: the 2 ch at the end of the row do not count as sts, they are only used to turn the work.

Row 1: work 14 ch, then starting in third ch from hook, 1 htr in each st across, 2 ch, turn (12 sts).
Rows 2–7: 1 htr in each st across, 2 ch, turn (12 sts).
Row 8: 1 htr in each st across (12 sts).
Cut yarn and weave in ends.

Ear (make two)

Use yarn (O).
Round 1: 6 dc into a MR (6 sts).
Round 2: 2 dc in each st around (12 sts).
Join round with 1 sl st and fasten off, leaving a long tail for making up *(see photo 15)*.

Ruff

Use yarn (R).
Worked in rows.
Row 1: work 12 ch, then starting in third ch from hook, 3 htr in each st across the chain (30 sts).
Leave a long tail of yarn for sewing up.

Sew the comforter under the head in the opening of round 11.
Fasten off and weave in ends.
Embroider the eyes (in French knots) using black embroidery thread between rounds 5 and 6, 3 sts apart and the nose using yarn (G) between rounds 6 and 7.
Sew the ears to the head at round 3.
Tie the ruff around the cuddly toy's neck.
Cut yarn and weave in ends into the head *(see photo 16)*.

15

16

Birthday cake

Use yarns (X), (V), (R), (G) and (L) and a small cardboard circle.

Cake

Stuff cake as you go.
Use yarn (X).
Round 1: 6 dc into a MR (6 sts).
Round 2: 2 dc in each st around (12 sts).
Round 3: (1 dc, 2 dc in the next st) six times (18 sts).
Round 4: (2 dc, 2 dc in the next st) six times (24 sts).
Round 5: (3 dc, 2 dc in the next st) six times (30 sts).
Round 6: (4 dc, 2 dc in the next st) six times (36 sts).
Round 7: (5 dc, 2 dc in the next st) six times (42 sts).
Round 8: (6 dc, 2 dc in the next st) six times (48 sts).
Round 9: 1 dc in blo of each st around (48 sts).
Rounds 10 and 11: 1 dc in each st around (48 sts).
Slip a cardboard circle into the bottom of the cake to give it a more stable base.
Continue using yarn (V).
Round 12: 1 dc in each st around (48 sts) *(see photo 17)*.
Continue using yarn (X).
Rounds 13–16: 1 dc in each st around (48 sts). Finish with 1 sl st and keep a length of yarn for sewing together.

Icing

Use yarn (R).
Round 1: 6 dc into a MR (6 sts).
Round 2: 2 dc in each st around (12 sts).
Round 3: (1 dc, 2 dc in the next st) six times (18 sts).
Round 4: (2 dc, 2 dc in the next st) six times (24 sts).
Round 5: (3 dc, 2 dc in the next st) six times (30 sts).
Round 6: (4 dc, 2 dc in the next st) six times (36 sts).
Round 7: (5 dc, 2 dc in the next st) six times (42 sts).
Round 8: (6 dc, 2 dc in the next st) six times (48 sts).
Round 9: 4 dc in flo of each st around (192 sts).
Finish with 1 sl st.
Cut yarn and weave in end *(see photo 18)*.

Candle

Use yarn (G).

Round 1: 6 dc into a MR (6 sts).
Round 2: 1 dc in blo of each st around (6 sts).
Rounds 3–7: 1 dc in each st around (6 sts). Stuff, or slip a little cylinder of rolled-up paper inside the candle.
Fasten off and sew up the opening with a darning needle.
Weave in ends.

Flame

Use yarn (L).

Row 1: work 4 ch, then starting in second ch from hook, 1 sl st, 1 dc, 1 sl st along chain (3 sts).
Fasten off to secure, leaving enough yarn for making up.

Sew the flame to the top of the candle.

Cut yarn and weave in ends.

Sew the candle to the centre of the cake and embroider little multi-coloured sprinkles on the icing. Finish stuffing the cake, then put a cardboard circle on top to make it more stable. Place the icing on the cake and sew it in place, passing the yarn through blo of the sts of the icing and flo of the sts of the cake.

Cut yarn and weave in ends *(see photo 19)*.

Sweets (make one in each colour)

Use yarns (G), (F), (Z) and (C).

Ball

Round 1: 6 dc into a MR (6 sts).
Round 2: 2 dc in each st around (12 sts).
Rounds 3–5: 1 dc in each st around (12 sts).
Round 6: 6 dc2tog (6 sts).
Stuff.

Fasten off and sew up the opening, passing the yarn through flo of the sts of round 9.

Weave in ends and cut remaining yarn.

Wrapper (make two per sweet)

Round 1: working into a MR, 1 sl st, 2 ch (counts as first tr), then 9 tr (10 sts); close round with 1 sl st into top of ch.
Fasten off, leaving enough yarn for making up.

Using a darning needle, weave the yarn through the tr to the centre. Pull on the starting yarn and knot the 2 tails together. Sew the wrappers on each side of the ball at rounds 1 and 6.

Weave in ends *(see photo 20)*.

17

18

19

20

The
Twins

Pompom the rabbit is never far away either!

Side by side ever since their arrival in the world, Charlie and Penny are inseparable. Whether at home, in the park, at school or on holiday, they are never apart! This afternoon, they plan to draw a pretty picture for their little sister Susan's birthday and make some bunting for the occasion.

Charlie

THE BOY TWIN

Finished height: 18cm (7in)

You will need

DMC Natura Just Cotton (4-ply/fingering) yarn, 50g/1¾oz/155m/170yd, in (R), (P), (A), (L) and (H) and a little of yarns (F), (E), (X), (C), (M), (K) and (O)
DMC Merino Essentiel 3 (4-ply/fingering) yarn, 50g/1¾oz/200m/218yd, in (DD)
Hobbii Diablo (1–3-ply/lace weight) yarn, 50g/1¾oz/225m/246yd, in (HH), for the hair (it is also possible to use DMC Natura Just Cotton – see page 17)
Dark brown (or black) and rust embroidery thread
2.25mm (UK 13, US B1) crochet hook, 3mm (UK 11, US 2/3) crochet hook only for the hair
4 small buttons and a piece of stiff cardboard
Basic tools and materials (see pages 10–12)

Making the doll

Note: unless stated otherwise, always work in spiral rounds using a 2.25mm (UK 13, US B1) crochet hook.

Body

Note: start with the legs.

Leg (make two)

Use yarns (P), (A) and (R).

Stuff legs as you go. Start using yarn (P).

Round 1: 6 dc into a MR (6 sts).
Round 2: 2 dc in each st around (12 sts).
Rounds 3–5: 1 dc in each st around (12 sts).
Round 6: 4 dc, 2 dc2tog, 4 dc (10 sts).
Rounds 7–9: 1 dc in each st around (10 sts), changing to yarn (A) on last yrh.
Round 10: 1 dc in blo of each st around (10 sts).
Rounds 11–26: 1 dc in each st around (10 sts); work an additional 6 or 7 dc to reach the side of the leg.
Finish with 1 sl st.

Cut yarn and weave in ends. Finish stuffing.

Crochet second leg in same way as far as round 25. Crochet another 2 or 3 dc to reach inside of leg, changing to yarn (R) on last yrh.

Round 26: 1 dc in each st around (10 sts) *(see photo 1)*. Do not cut yarn but continue as follows:

Body

Use yarns (R), (L) and (A). Stuff body as you go.

Lay the two legs side by side, toes up and after second leg, work 4 ch and join to first leg with 1 dc (counts as first dc of round).

Round 1: 1 dc in each of 10 sts around first leg, 1 dc in 4 sts of ch, 1 dc in each of 10 sts of the other leg and 1 dc in 4 sts on other side of ch (10 + 4 + 10 + 4 = 28 sts) *(see photo 2)*.
Place stitch marker here (it will be on doll's front).
Rounds 2–6: 1 dc in each st around (28 sts).
Round 7: crochet 20 dc to reach left side, changing to yarn (L) on last yrh to make the sweater (20 sts).
Move stitch marker.

Note: always change yarn colour on the last yrh of the round in question. Leave the unused yarn hanging on the wrong side of the work, continue with the new colour, then pick up the waiting yarn at the stated round.

Round 8: 1 dc in blo of each st around (28 sts). Continue using yarn (R).

1

2

Rounds 9 and 10: 1 dc in each st around (28 sts). Continue using yarn (L).
Round 11: (5 dc, dc2tog) four times (24 sts). Continue using yarn (R).
Round 12: 1 dc in each st around (24 sts).
Round 13: (4 dc, dc2tog) four times (20 sts); work another 1 dc and move the stitch marker to centre the joins on the side. Continue using yarn (L).
Round 14: 1 dc in each st around (20 sts). Continue using yarn (R).
Round 15: (3 dc, dc2tog) four times (16 sts).
Round 16: 1 dc in each st around (16 sts). Continue using yarn (L).
Round 17: (2 dc, dc2tog) four times (12 sts); work 1 dc (start of new round), changing to yarn (A) on last yrh. Cut yarn and knot the other tails.
Round 18: 1 dc in blo of each st around (12 sts).
Rounds 19 and 20: 1 dc in each st around (12 sts).
Finish stuffing the body.

Do not cut yarn but continue directly with head *(see photo 3)*.

Head

Use yarn (A).

Stuff head as you go.

Round 1: 2 dc in each st around (24 sts).
Round 2: (1 dc, 2 dc in the next st) twelve times (36 sts).
Round 3: (5 dc, 2 dc in the next st) six times (42 sts).
Round 4: 3 dc, 2 dc in the next st, (6 dc, 2 dc in the next st) five times, 3 dc (48 sts).

Note: to make the neck more stable, slip a pipe cleaner (chenille stick) into the opening *(see photo 4)*.

Rounds 5–10: 1 dc in each st around (48 sts).
Round 11: (14 dc, dc2tog) three times (45 sts).
Rounds 12–15: 1 dc in each st around (45 sts).
Round 16: (13 dc, dc2tog) three times (42 sts).
Round 17: 1 dc in each st around (42 sts).
Round 18: (5 dc, dc2tog) six times (36 sts).
Round 19: (4 dc, dc2tog) six times (30 sts).
Round 20: (3 dc, dc2tog) six times (24 sts).
Round 21: (2 dc, dc2tog) six times (18 sts).
Round 22: (1 dc, dc2tog) six times (12 sts).
Round 23: 6 dc2tog (6 sts).
Cut a length of yarn.

Finish stuffing. Sew up the opening with the darning needle, passing the needle through flo of the sts of the last round to pull tight. Weave in end.

3

4

Project continues overleaf

Arm (make two)

Crocheted separately using yarns (A), (R) and (L).
Start with yarn (A).
Round 1: 6 dc into a MR (6 sts).
Round 2: (2 dc, 2 dc in the next st) twice (8 sts).
Rounds 3–5: 1 dc in each st around (8 sts).
Round 6: (2 dc, dc2tog) twice (6 sts).
Round 7: 1 dc in each st around (6 sts). Stuff hand lightly (using a wooden skewer or crochet hook handle to help). Continue using yarn (R).
Rounds 8 and 9: 1 dc in each st around (6 sts). Continue using yarn (L).
Round 10: 1 dc in each st around (6 sts). Continue using yarn (R).
Rounds 11 and 12: 1 dc in each st around (6 sts). Continue using yarn (L).
Round 13: 1 dc in each st around (6 sts). Continue using yarn (R).
Rounds 14 and 15: 1 dc in each st around (6 sts). Continue using yarn (L).
Round 16: 1 dc in each st around (6 sts). Continue using yarn (R).
Rounds 17 and 18: 1 dc in each st around (6 sts).
Pinch top of arm together, ensuring that the joins are positioned in the middle of the arm (add or omit 1 dc if necessary) and sew up with 3 dc into sts on both sides at same time.
Cut, leaving sufficient yarn for making up.

Sew the arms on either side of the body, at round 17 *(see photo 5)*.

Hair

Use Hobbii Diablo yarn (HH) – 3mm (UK 11, US 2/3) crochet hook.

Note: it is also possible to use cotton yarn (see page 17).

Round 1: 6 dc into a MR (6 sts).
Round 2: 2 dc in each st around (12 sts).
Round 3: (1 dc, 2 dc in the next st) six times (18 sts).
Round 4: (2 dc, 2 dc in the next st) six times (24 sts).
Round 5: (3 dc, 2 dc in the next st) six times (30 sts).
Round 6: (4 dc, 2 dc in the next st) six times (36 sts).
Round 7: (5 dc, 2 dc in the next st) six times (42 sts).
Round 8: (6 dc, 2 dc in the next st) six times (48 sts).
Rounds 9–20: 1 dc in each st around (48 sts).
(The number of rounds can be adapted depending on the yarn used and your own crocheting style. Try the hairpiece before you work the last round.)
Do not cut yarn, but continue crocheting strands all around the hairpiece as follows:
Round 21: 1 sl st, then (5 ch, 1 sl st in the next st). 34 times, crocheting the 5 ch directly after the sl st (34 little strands).
Continue with the fringe: 1 dc, 1 htr, 10 tr, 1 htr, 1 sl st.
Leave a long tail of yarn for sewing up. Adjust the hairpiece on the head, positioning the fringe on the forehead *(see photo 6)*, then sew into place working into the sts of round 20 among the little strands and row 21 for the fringe. Cut yarn and weave in end.

5

6

7

8

9

> *Tip*
> ***Gently brush the hair with a little metal brush to make the fibres stand out.***

Use dark brown (or black) embroidery thread to embroider the eyes at round 8, spacing them 8 sts apart. Embroider some freckles under the eyes using the rust embroidery thread *(see photo 7)*.

Dungarees

Use yarn (H).

Start with the waist.

Round 1: work 34 ch, then join with 1 dc into first ch (counts as first st of round), ensuring that the chain is not twisted and work 1 dc in each st around (34 sts).
Rounds 2 and 3: 1 dc in each st around (34 sts).
Round 4: 8 dc, 2 dc in the next st, 16 dc, 2 dc in the next st, 8 dc (36 sts).
Rounds 5–10: 1 dc in each st around (36 sts).
Mark the mid-point between the legs. Allow 17 sts for each leg.

Note: 1 dc remains free on either side of mid-point (mark with pins) *(see photo 8).*

Join the last st of the back to the first st of the front with 1 dc (counts as first dc of round). The sts of first leg now form a round *(see photo 9)*. Continue working as follows:
Rounds 11–23: 1 dc in each st around (17 sts).
Round 24: (to form the turn-up). 1 dc in flo of each st around (17 sts). Finish with 1 sl st.
Fasten off and sew the turn-up in place with a few stitches. Weave in end.

Second leg: join yarn at back of work, next to pin and work 1 dc in each of next 17 sts (17 sts). Join in a round and rep rounds 12 to 24 (17 sts).
Finish with 1 sl st. Fasten off and sew the turn-up in place with a few stitches. Weave in end. Sew up opening between legs with a needle. Weave in end.

10

11

Bib (top of dungarees)

Use yarn (H).

Worked in rows.

Identify the central 8 sts on the front of the dungarees and join the yarn in the first of these 8 sts.
Row 1: 1 dc in each st, 1 ch and turn (8 sts).
Row 2: 1 dc in each st (8 sts).

Note: for the following rows, turn the work but do not use a starting chain, so that the start is angled.

Row 3: 1 dc in each st (7 sts).
Row 4: 1 dc in each st (6 sts).
Row 5: 1 dc in each st (5 sts).
Without cutting the yarn, work 16 ch for the first shoulder strap, then crochet 15 sl st along the chain and 5 dc on the left side of the bib. Finish with 1 sl st in the foundation chain (waist). Cut yarn and weave in end.
Continue on the other side, starting at the bottom of the bib: join the yarn and work 5 dc along the bib, then 16 ch for the second strap. Work 15 sl st along the chain. Fasten off and sew to the top of the bib with the darning needle, then weave in ends.

Cross the shoulder straps to the back of the dungarees and sew on. Weave in remaining ends *(see photo 10)*.
Embroider a little pocket in backstitch using yarn (P) *(see photo 11)*.

Garment variation: use the colour of your choice. For short legs, only crochet 4 rounds after row 11, then cut yarn and weave in ends.

For Penny's dungaree dress, work rows 1 to 10 of the dungarees, cut the yarn and weave in ends, then follow the instructions for the bib and braces.

Project continues overleaf

Shoe (make two)

Use yarns (X) and (L) *(see photo 12)*.
Start with the sole using yarn (X).
Round 1: 7 dc into a MR (7 sts).
Round 2: 2 dc in each st around (14 sts).
Round 3: 2 dc in each of the next 2 sts, 3 dc, 2 dc in each of the next 4 sts, 3 dc, 2 dc in each the next 2 sts (22 sts).
Round 4: 1 dc in blo of each st around (22 sts), changing to yarn (L) on last yrh.
Rounds 5 and 6: 1 dc in each st around (22 sts).
Round 7: 7 dc, 4 dc2tog, 7 dc (18 sts).
Round 8: 6 dc, 3 dc2tog, 6 dc (15 sts).
Round 9: 1 dc in each st around (15 sts).
Finish with 1 sl st.

Cut yarn and weave in ends.

Embroider 2 little lines using yarn (X) on the front of the shoe for the laces.

Hat

Using Merino Essentiel 3 yarn (DD).

Worked in rows, in blo of sts.

Note: the 1 ch at the end of the row does not count as a stitch; it is only used to turn the work.

Row 1: work 23 ch (adjust depending on size of doll) and work 1 dc in each st across (starting in second ch from hook), 1 ch, turn (22 sts).
Rows 2–52: 1 dc in blo of each st across (rib effect), 1 ch, turn (22 sts).
Row 53: 1 dc in blo of each st across (22 sts) *(see photo 13)*.

Note: number of rows can be adapted to size of doll's head.

Fasten off, leaving enough yarn for sewing the two long sides of the rectangle together to form a cylinder. Weave the yarn, from front to back, through the sts of the top of hat and draw tight to close the opening *(see photo 14)*. Fasten off and weave in ends. Make a pompom (using the yarn of your choice), approximately 4cm (1½in) in diameter and sew it on to the hat *(see photo 15)*.

12

13

14

15

Making the accessories (see photos 16 and 17)

Balloon

Use yarn (M).

Stuff balloon as you go.

Round 1: 6 dc into a MR (6 sts).
Round 2: 2 dc in each st around (12 sts).
Round 3: (1 dc, 2 dc in the next st) six times (18 sts).
Round 4: (2 dc, 2 dc in the next st) six times (24 sts).
Round 5: 1 dc in each st around (24 sts).
Round 6: (3 dc, 2 dc in the next st) six times (30 sts).
Rounds 7–11: 1 dc in each st around (30 sts).
Round 12: (3 dc, dc2tog) six times (24 sts).
Round 13: 1 dc in each st around (24 sts).
Round 14: (2 dc, dc2tog) six times (18 sts).
Round 15: 1 dc in each st around (18 sts).
Round 16: (1 dc, dc2tog) six times (12 sts).
Round 17: 1 dc in each st around (12 sts).
Round 18: 6 dc2tog (6 sts).
Round 19: (1 sl st, 1 ch, 1 htr) in the same st, then two htr in each st around (12 sts). Finish with 1 sl st into first ch of round.
Cut the yarn, leaving enough yarn for making up. Using a darning needle, draw the bottom tight (at round 18), then fasten off. Bring the yarn out in the centre for the string.

The bunting

Use yarns (F), (L), (M), (C) and (K).

Work one pennant in each colour, in rows, from the tip upwards.

Note: the 1 ch at the end of the row does not count as a stitch; it is only used to turn the work.

Row 1: 2 ch, then starting in second ch from hook, 2 dc in each st across, 1 ch, turn (2 sts).
Row 2: 1 dc, 2 dc in the next st, 1 ch, turn (3 sts).
Row 3: 2 dc, 2 dc in the next st, 1 ch, turn (4 sts).
Row 4: 3 dc, 2 dc in the next st, 1 ch, turn (5 sts).
Row 5: 4 dc, 2 dc in the next st, 1 ch, turn (6 sts).
Row 6: 5 dc, 2 dc in the next st, 1 ch, turn (7 sts).
Row 7: 6 dc, 2 dc in the next st, 1 ch, turn (8 sts).
Row 8: 7 dc, 2 dc in the next st, 1 ch, turn (9 sts).
Row 9: 8 dc, 2 dc in the next st, 1 ch, turn (10 sts).
Row 10: 9 dc, 2 dc in the next st (11 sts).
Cut yarn and thread the yarn through the loop to secure.
Weave in ends.

16

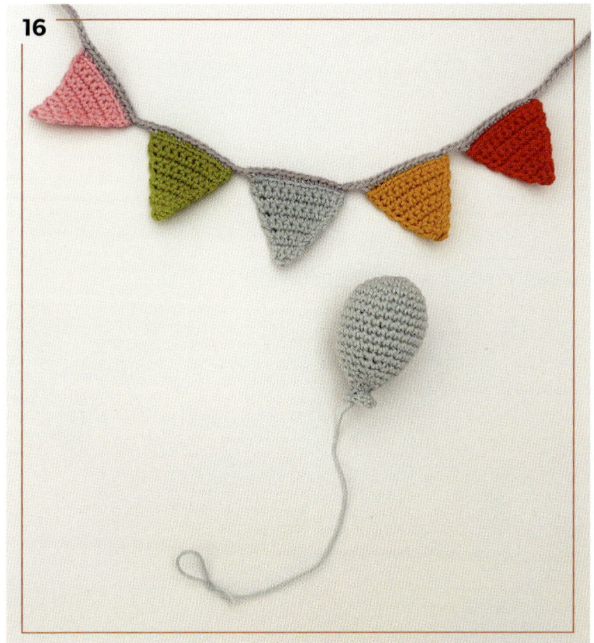

17

Ribbon

Use yarn (O).

Work 20 ch, then join to first pennant and work 11 dc in blo of sts of last row, 3 ch, 11 dc in blo of second pennant. Continue in the same way to end of fifth pennant. 20 ch to finish.

Cut yarn and thread the yarn through the loop to secure.

Weave in ends.

Project continues overleaf

Pompom the rabbit *(see photo 18)*

Use yarns (R) and (L).

Head

Use yarn (R).

Stuff head as you go.

Round 1: 6 dc into a MR (6 sts).
Round 2: 2 dc in each st around (12 sts).
Round 3: 1 dc in each st around (12 sts).
Round 4: (1 dc, 2 dc in the next st) six times (18 sts).
Rounds 5–8: 1 dc in each st around (18 sts).
Round 9: (1 dc, dc2tog) six times (12 sts).
Round 10: 6 dc2tog (6 sts).
Cut a length of yarn and sew up the opening with the darning needle, passing the needle through flo of the sts. Pull tight and work in the end of the yarn.

Ear (make two)

Use yarn (R).

Work 6 ch.

Note: sts will be crocheted on both sides of chain.

Round 1: starting in second ch from hook, 1 sl st, 1 dc, 1 htr, 1 dc, 3 dc in first ch; continue on other side. 1 dc, 1 htr, 1 dc, 1 sl st (11 sts). Cut a length of yarn to sew the ears to round 7 of the head, spacing them 2 sts apart.
Weave in ends.

Embroider French knots for the two little black eyes on round 5, spacing them 5 sts apart; and the nose on round 1.

Body

Use yarn (R).

Stuff body as you go.

Round 1: 6 dc into a MR (6 sts).
Round 2: 2 dc in each st around (12 sts).
Round 3: (1 dc, 2 dc in the next st) six times (18 sts).
Round 4: (1 dc, 2 dc in the next st) three times, 6 dc, (1 dc, 2 dc in the next st) three times (24 sts).
Rounds 5 and 6: 1 dc in each st around (24 sts).
Round 7: 4 dc2tog, 12 dc, 2 dc2tog (18 sts).
Round 8: 2 dc2tog, 5 dc, dc2tog, 7 dc (15 sts).
Round 9: (1 dc, dc2tog) five times (10 sts).
Cut a length of yarn then sew the body under the head: at the chin, weave the yarn between the sts of the body rather than through the loops of the last round, to pull the head down slightly. Fasten off and weave in ends.

Tail

Use yarn (R).

Round 1: 8 dc into a MR (8 sts).
Round 2: 1 dc in each st around (8 sts).
Round 3: (2 dc, dc2tog) twice (6 sts).
Join the circle with 1 sl st in the starting st, then fasten off leaving enough yarn for sewing the tail to the base of the back. Fasten off and weave in end.

18

Collar

Use yarn (L).

Work 14 ch, knot around the neck then secure the ends inside the body.

The wagon

Use yarn (F), a little of yarn (E), a piece of cardboard and four buttons.

Base (make two)

Work 9 ch.

Note: sts will be crocheted on both sides of chain.

Round 1: starting in second ch from hook, 7 dc, 3 dc in first ch; continue on other side. 6 dc, 2 dc in the next st (18 sts).
Round 2: 3 dc in the next st, 6 dc, 3 dc in the next st, 1 dc, 3 dc in the next st, 6 dc, 3 dc in the next st, 1 dc (26 sts).

Note: there will be one group of 3 dc at each corner.

Round 3: 1 dc, 3 dc in the next st, 8 dc, 3 dc in the next st, 3 dc, 3 dc in the next st, 8 dc, 3 dc in the next st, 2 dc (34 sts).
Round 4: 2 dc, 3 dc in the next st, 10 dc, 3 dc in the next st, 5 dc, 3 dc in the next st, 10 dc, 3 dc in the next st, 3 dc (42 sts).
Fasten off and weave in ends.

Do not cut the yarn from the second base piece but continue directly with the edges.

Cut a small piece of cardboard the size of the floor of the wagon and gently round off the corners *(see photo 19)*.

The edges

Position the two bases face to face, wrong sides together and working in the blo of the stitches opposite each other:

Round 5: 1 dc in blo of each st around (insert the cardboard between the two base pieces before finishing the round). (42 sts) *(see photo 20)*.

Rounds 6–9: 1 dc in each st around (42 sts).

Finish with 1 sl st.

Cut yarn and weave in ends.

Pull ring

Use yarn (E).

Work 5 ch, then starting in second ch from hook, 4 dc (4 sts). Cut yarn and fasten off to secure.

Fold the pull ring in half and fasten off to secure.

Weave in ends. Thread a length of yarn (F) into the ring for the pull string.

Sew two buttons on each side of the wagon at round 5.

19

20

Penny

THE GIRL TWIN

Finished height: 18cm (7in)

You will need

DMC Natura Just Cotton (4-ply/fingering) yarn, 50g/1¾oz/155m/170yd, in (R), (E), (B), (A), (U) and (O) and a little of yarns (Q), (AA) and (J)

Hobbii Diablo (1–3-ply/lace weight) yarn, 50g/1¾oz/225m/246yd, in (HH), for the hair (it is also possible to use DMC Natura Just Cotton – see page 17)

A little red, green and yellow cotton (or embroidery thread) for the picture, dark brown (or black) and rust embroidery thread

2.25mm (UK 13, US B1) crochet hook, 3mm (UK 11, US 2/3) crochet hook only for the hair

Basic tools and materials (see pages 10–12)

Making the doll

Note: unless stated otherwise, always work in spiral rounds using a 2.25mm (UK 13, US B1) crochet hook.

1

2

Body

Note: start with the legs.

Leg (make two)

Use yarns (U) and (R).

Stuff legs as you go.

Note: always change yarn colour on the last yrh of the round in question. Leave the unused yarn hanging on the wrong side of the work, continue with the new colour, then take up waiting yarn at the stated round.

3

Start with yarn (U).
Round 1: 6 dc into a MR (6 sts).
Round 2: 2 dc in each st around (12 sts).
Rounds 3–5: 1 dc in each st around (12 sts).
Round 6: 4 dc, 2 dc2tog, 4 dc (10 sts).
Round 7: 1 dc in each st around (10 sts), changing to yarn (R) on last yrh.
Rounds 8 and 9: 1 dc in each st around (10 sts), changing to yarn (U) on last yrh.
Rounds 10 and 11: 1 dc in each st around (10 sts); work an additional 1 dc and move the stitch marker to centre the joins on the side.
Continue using yarn (R).
Rounds 12 and 13: 1 dc in each st around (10 sts).
Continue using yarn (U).
Rounds 14 and 15: 1 dc in each st around (10 sts). 1 dc (new start of round).
Continue using yarn (R).
Rounds 16 and 17: 1 dc in each st around (10 sts).
Continue using yarn (U).
Rounds 18 and 19: 1 dc in each st around (10 sts). 1 dc (new start of row).
Continue using yarn (R).
Rounds 20 and 21: 1 dc in each st around (10 sts).
Continue using yarn (U).
Rounds 22 and 23: 1 dc in each st around (10 sts). 1 dc (new start of row).
Continue using yarn (R).
Rounds 24 and 25: 1 dc in each st around (10 sts).
Continue using yarn (U).
Round 26: 1 dc in each st around (10 sts); work an additional 3 dc to reach side of leg.
Finish with 1 sl st.

Cut yarn and weave in ends. Finish stuffing.

4

5

Crochet second leg in same way as far as round 25.
Round 26: 1 dc in next 8 sts (8 sts), to reach mid-point between the legs *(see photo 1)*.
Do not cut the yarn but continue as follows:

Body

Use yarns (U), (O) and (A).
Stuff body as you go. Lay the two legs side by side, toes up and after second leg, work 4 ch and join to first leg with 1 dc (counts as first dc of round).
Round 1: 1 dc in each of 10 sts around first leg, 1 dc in 4 sts of chain, 1 dc in each of 10 sts of the other leg and 1 dc in 4 sts on other side of chain (10 + 4 + 10 + 4 = 28 sts) *(see photo 2)*.
Place stitch marker here (it will be on doll's front).
Rounds 2–6: 1 dc in each st around (28 sts).
Round 7: crochet 20 dc to reach left side, changing to yarn (O) on last yrh to make the sweater (20 sts).
Move stitch marker.
Round 8: 1 dc in blo of each st around (28 sts).
Rounds 9 and 10: 1 dc in each st around (28 sts).
Round 11: (5 dc, dc2tog) four times (24 sts).
Round 12: 1 dc in each st around (24 sts).
Round 13: (4 dc, dc2tog) four times (20 sts).
Round 14: 1 dc in each st around (20 sts).
Round 15: (3 dc, dc2tog) four times (16 sts).
Round 16: 1 dc in each st around (16 sts).
Round 17: (2 dc, dc2tog) four times (12 sts); work 1 dc (new start of round). changing to yarn (A) on last yrh *(see photo 3)*.
Round 18: 1 dc in blo of each st around (12 sts).
Rounds 19 and 20: 1 dc in each st around (12 sts). Finish stuffing the body. Do not cut yarn but continue directly with the head.

Head

Use yarn (A).
Stuff head as you go.
Round 1: 2 dc in each st around (24 sts).
Round 2: (1 dc, 2 dc in the next st) twelve times (36 sts).
Round 3: (5 dc, 2 dc in the next st) six times (42 sts).
Round 4: 3 dc, 2 dc in the next st, (6 dc, 2 dc in the next st) five times, 3 dc (48 sts).

Note: to make the neck more stable, slip a pipe cleaner (chenille stick) into the opening *(see photo 4)*.

Rounds 5–10: 1 dc in each st around (48 sts).
Round 11: (14 dc, dc2tog) three times (45 sts).
Rounds 12–15: 1 dc in each st around (45 sts).
Round 16: (13 dc, dc2tog) three times (42 sts).
Round 17: 1 dc in each st around (42 sts).
Round 18: (5 dc, dc2tog) six times (36 sts).
Round 19: (4 dc, dc2tog) six times (30 sts).
Round 20: (3 dc, dc2tog) six times (24 sts).
Round 21: (2 dc, dc2tog) six times (18 sts).
Round 22: (1 dc, dc2tog) six times (12 sts).
Round 23: 6 dc2tog (6 sts).
Fasten off, leaving a length of yarn for sewing. Finish stuffing and sew up the opening with the darning needle, passing the needle through flo of the sts of the last round to pull tight.
Weave in ends *(see photo 5)*.

Arm (make two)

Crocheted separately using yarns (A) and (O).
Start with yarn (A).
Round 1: 6 dc into a MR (6 sts).
Round 2: (2 dc, 2 dc in the next st) twice (8 sts).
Rounds 3–5: 1 dc in each st around (8 sts).
Round 6: (2 dc, dc2tog) twice (6 sts).
Round 7: 1 dc in each st around (6 sts).
Stuff hand lightly (using a wooden skewer or crochet hook handle to help).
Continue using yarn (O).
Rounds 8–18: 1 dc in each st around (6 sts). Pinch top of arm together and sew up with 3 dc into sts on both sides at same time. Cut, leaving sufficient yarn for making up. Sew the arms on either side of the body, at round 17 *(see photo 6)*.

Project continues overleaf

Hair

Use Hobbii Diablo yarn (HH) – 3mm (UK 11, US 2/3) crochet hook.

Note: it is also possible to use cotton yarn (see page 17).

Hairpiece

Round 1: 6 dc into a MR (6 sts).
Round 2: 2 dc in each st around (12 sts).
Round 3: (1 dc, 2 dc in the next st) six times (18 sts).
Round 4: (2 dc, 2 dc in the next st) six times (24 sts).
Round 5: (3 dc, 2 dc in the next st) six times (30 sts).
Round 6: (4 dc, 2 dc in the next st) six times (36 sts).
Round 7: (5 dc, 2 dc in the next st) six times (42 sts).
Round 8: (6 dc, 2 dc in the next st) six times (48 sts).
Rounds 9–21: 1 dc in each st around (48 sts). (The number of rounds can be adapted depending on the yarn used and your own crocheting style. Try the hairpiece before you work the last round.)
Round 22: 10 dc, 18 htr, sk 1 st, 1 sl st. Do not work the other sts.
Leave a long tail of yarn for sewing up.

Adjust the hairpiece on the head, positioning the sl st to the left of the forehead *(see photo 7)*. Hold in place with pins.

Braids

Cut 18 strands, each 25cm (10in) in length (nine strands for each braid).

Mark the position of the braids on either side of the hairpiece. Using the crochet hook, pull the lengths through the relevant st of the last round and fold in half *(see photo 8)*. Plait the braids and tie the ends with a strand of yarn. Trim the ends evenly with a pair of scissors. Sew the hairpiece to the head *(see photo 9)*. following the sts of the last round.

Cut yarn and weave in end.

Knot or embroider a few strands on the forehead.

> ***Tip***
> ***Gently brush the hair with a little metal brush to make the fibres stand out.***

Use dark brown embroidery thread (or black). to embroider the eyes at round 8, spacing them 8 sts apart. Embroider some freckles under the eyes using the rust embroidery thread *(see photo 10)*.

7

8

9

10

Dress

Use yarn (B).

Start with the waist.

Round 1: work 34 ch, then join with 1 dc into first ch (counts as first st of round), ensuring that the chain is not twisted) and work 1 dc in each st around (34 sts).
Rounds 2 and 3: 1 dc in each st around (34 sts).
Round 4: 2 htr in each st around (68 sts).
Rounds 5–9: 1 htr in each st around (68 sts).
Finish the work with 1 dc and 1 sl st to equal out the round.

Do not cut yarn but continue the picot st around the bottom of the skirt as follows: *2 ch, 1 sl st in next st*, rep this sequence all around the skirt, then cut and weave in ends.

Shoulder straps

Join yarn at back of work at waist level (on starting st of round 1, in first chain of round 1), work dc in 14 sts round waist. Work the first shoulder strap: 21 ch, starting in second ch from hook, dc along chain. Work 1 dc in the next st of the waist to secure. Continue with 4 dc, then work the second strap in exactly the same way. Work 1 dc in the next st of the waist to secure and finish with 14 dc. Join with 1 sl st to equal out the round, then cut yarn and weave in ends.

Sew the shoulder straps to the back of the skirt.

Weave in remaining ends *(see photos 11 and 12)*.

Garment variation: use the colour of your choice. To make a dungaree dress, work rounds 1 to 10 of Charlie's dungarees *(see instructions on page 75)*.

Ankle boots (make two)

Use yarns (E) and (R).

Start with the sole using yarn (E).

Round 1: 7 dc into a MR (7 sts).
Round 2: 2 dc in each st around (14 sts).
Round 3: 2 dc in the next 2 sts, 3 dc, 2 dc in the next 4 sts, 3 dc, 2 dc in the next 2 sts (22 sts), changing to yarn (R) on last yrh.
Round 4: 1 dc in blo of each st around (22 sts).
Continue using yarn (E).

Rounds 5 and 6: 1 dc in each st around (22 sts).
Round 7: 7 dc, 4 dc2tog, 7 dc (18 sts).
Round 8: 6 dc, 3 dc2tog, 6 dc (15 sts).
Rounds 9 and 10: 1 dc in each st around (15 sts).
Continue using yarn (R).

Round 11: 1 dc in blo of each st around (15 sts).
Finish with 1 sl st. Fasten off and weave in ends *(see photo 13)*.

11

12

13

Project continues overleaf

Making the accessories (see photo 14)

Teddy-bear handbag

Use yarns (E) and (R).

The bag consists of two circles which will then be sewn together: one with a teddy-bear face, the other plain.

Teddy-bear circle

Use yarn (E).

Round 1: 6 dc into a MR (6 sts).
Round 2: 2 dc in each st around (12 sts).
Round 3: (1 dc, 2 dc in the next st) six times (18 sts).
Round 4: (2 dc, 2 dc in the next st) six times (24 sts).
Finish with 1 sl st. Fasten off and weave in end.

Muzzle

Use yarn (R).

6 dc into a MR (6 sts).

Join the round with 1 sl st and leave a long tail of yarn to sew the muzzle to the circle. Embroider the nose and eyes in French knots using a dark-coloured yarn. Weave in ends.

Ear (make two)

Use yarn (E).

6 dc into a MR (6 sts). Join the round with 1 sl st.

Pull the ring tight, leave a long tail of yarn, then sew the ears to each side of the bag.

Weave in ends.

Plain circle

Use yarn (E).

Round 1: 6 dc into a MR (6 sts).
Round 2: 2 dc in each st around (12 sts).
Round 3: (1 dc, 2 dc in the next st) six times (18 sts).
Round 4: (2 dc, 2 dc in the next st) six times (24 sts).
Do not cut yarn; continue directly with the side of the bag: 1 sl st, 1 ch, then 16 dc in blo of sts from round 4.

Leave a long tail of yarn for sewing up.

Sew the two circles together, passing the yarn through flo of the sts of the teddy-bear circle and both loops of the sts of the plain circle, around the last 16 sts worked.

Fasten off and weave in ends.

Strap

Work 42 ch. Cut yarn and fasten off, then sew the strap to each side of the bag.

Weave in ends.

14

Picture

Use yarn (Q) and a little red, green, yellow and brown.

Worked in rows.

Note: the 1 ch at the end of the row does not count as a stitch; it is only used to turn the work.

Row 1: work 25 ch, then starting in the second ch from hook, 1 dc in each st across, 1 ch, turn (12 sts).
Rows 2–8: 1 dc in each st across, 1 ch, turn (12 sts).
Row 9: 1 dc in each st across (12 sts).
Cut yarn and weave in ends.

Embroider a 'drawing' using different coloured pieces of cotton or embroidery thread.

Cut yarn and weave in ends at the back.

If necessary, press the picture with an iron to flatten out.

Penny's doll

Use yarns (A), (J) and (AA) *(see photo 15)*.
Stuff as you go.
Start with the head, using yarn (A).
Round 1: 6 dc into a MR (6 sts).
Round 2: 2 dc in each st around (12 sts).
Round 3: (2 dc, 2 dc in the next st) four times (16 sts).
Round 4: (3 dc, 2 dc in the next st) four times (20 sts).
Rounds 5–8: 1 dc in each st around (20 sts).
Round 9: (3 dc, dc2tog) four times (16 sts).
Round 10: 8 dc2tog (8 sts).
Round 11: 1 dc in each st around (8 sts), changing to yarn (J) on last yrh.
Stuff the head.
Continue directly with the body:
Round 12: (1 dc, 2 dc in the next st) four times (12 sts).
Round 13: (2 dc, 2 dc in the next st) four times (16 sts).
Rounds 14 and 15: 1 dc in each st around (16 sts).
Round 16: 4 dc, 2 dc in the next st, 7 dc, 2 dc in the next st, 3 dc (18 sts).
Round 17: 1 dc in each st around (18 sts).
Round 18: (1 sl st, 2 ch) in each st around.
Finish with 1 sl st. Fasten off and weave in end.

Embroider the eyes in dark brown (or black) at round 8, spacing them 4 sts apart.

Arm (make two)

Use yarn (A).
Work 8 ch, then work 1 htr in third ch from hook, then 1 sl st in each st to end (6 sts). Fasten off, leaving a length of yarn, then sew the arms to the body.

Leg (make two)

Use yarn (A).
*Work 14 ch, then work 1 htr in third ch from hook, then 1 sl st in each st to end (12 sts). Do not cut yarn; rep from * immediately after first leg. Fasten off, leaving a length of yarn, then sew the legs to the bottom of the head, inside the dress *(see photo 16)*.

Hair

Use yarn (AA).
Round 1: 6 dc into a MR (6 sts).
Round 2: 2 dc in each st around (12 sts).
Round 3: (2 dc, 2 dc in the next st) four times (16 sts).
Round 4: (3 dc, 2 dc in the next st) four times (20 sts).
Rounds 5–8: 1 dc in each st around (20 sts).
Round 9: 4 dc, 1 sl st, 10 ch, 9 dc along the chain (starting in second ch from hook), 12 dc, 1 sl st, 10 ch, 9 dc along the chain, 3 dc.
Finish the work with 1 sl st and fasten off, leaving a long tail of yarn to sew the hair on to the head *(see photo 17)*.

15

16

17

The Grandparents

Jean and Lucie are very proud of their eldest daughter's wonderful family. They are looking forward to seeing them all gathered around their youngest granddaughter's birthday cake. Lucie has made her a pretty dress and Jean has wrapped the present. They are just about to arrive. If the weather is nice, they will play a game of boules (Jean's favourite pastime) in the garden and Lucie will be able to knit in the sun while chatting to her daughter. Nothing is more precious than sharing moments with family.

Jean

THE GRANDPA

Finished height: 27cm (10½in)

You will need

DMC Natura Just Cotton (4-ply/fingering) yarn, 50g/1¾oz/155m/170yd, in (I), (A), (R), (S), (BB) and (G) and a little of yarns (B), (AA), (X), (W), (E) and (F)
DMC Merino Essentiel 3 (4-ply/fingering) yarn, 50g/1¾oz/200m/218yd, in (EE)
Hobbii Diablo (1–3-ply/lace weight) yarn, 50g/1¾oz/225m/246yd, in (II) for the hair (it is also possible to use DMC Natura Just Cotton – see page 17)

Navy blue, dark brown (or black) embroidery thread
2.25mm (UK 13, US B1) crochet hook, 3.5mm (UK 9, US E4) crochet hook for the hair
Some newspaper and a piece of fairly stiff cardboard
A wooden bead, 1.5cm (½in) in diameter, for the jack
Basic tools and materials (see pages 10–12)

Special stitch:
3-treble bobble (3 tr for thumbs)

Making the doll

Note: unless stated otherwise, always work in spiral rounds using a 2.25mm (UK 13, US B1) crochet hook.

Body

Note: start with the legs.

Leg (make two)

Use yarns (I), (A) and (R).
Stuff as you go.
Start with yarn (I).
Work 7 ch.

Note: sts will be crocheted on both sides of chain.

Round 1: starting in second ch from hook, 5 dc, 3 dc in last ch; continue on other side. 4 dc, 2 dc in the next st (14 sts).
Round 2: 2 dc in the next st, 4 dc, 2 dc in next 3 sts, 5 dc, 2 dc in the next st (19 sts).
Rounds 3 and 4: 1 dc in each st around (19 sts).
Round 5: 7 dc, 3 dc2tog, 6 dc (16 sts).
Round 6: 6 dc, 2 dc2tog, 6 dc (14 sts).
Round 7: 5 dc, 2 dc2tog, 5 dc (12 sts).
Rounds 8–11: 1 dc in each st around (12 sts); work 1 more dc (to centre the joins on the back and move stitch marker), changing to yarn (A) on last yrh.
Round 12: 1 dc in blo in each st around (12 sts).
Round 13: 1 dc in each st around (12 sts) *(see photo 1)*.
Round 14: 2 dc in the next st, 11 dc (13 sts).
Rounds 15 and 16: 1 dc in each st around (13 sts).
Round 17: 2 dc, 2 dc in the next st, 10 dc (14 sts).
Rounds 18–21: 1 dc in each st around (14 sts).
Round 22: (2 dc in the next st, 6 dc) twice (16 sts).
Rounds 23–26: 1 dc in each st around (16 sts).
Round 27: 1 dc, 2 dc in the next st, 7 dc, 2 dc in the next st, 6 dc (18 sts).
Rounds 28–33: 1 dc in each st around (18 sts).
Round 34: 3 dc, 2 dc in the next st, 7 dc, 2 dc in the next st, 6 dc (20 sts).
Round 35: 1 dc in each st around (20 sts); work an additional 4 dc to reach the side of the leg.
Finish with 1 sl st.
Cut yarn and weave in ends. Finish stuffing.

Crochet second leg in same way as far as round 34.
Crochet another 4 dc to reach inside of leg, changing to yarn (R) on last yrh.
Round 35: 1 dc in each st around (20 sts) *(see photo 2)*. Do not cut yarn but continue as follows:

1

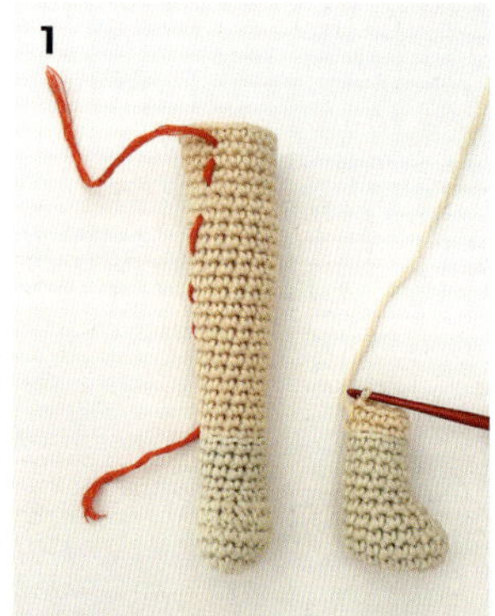

2

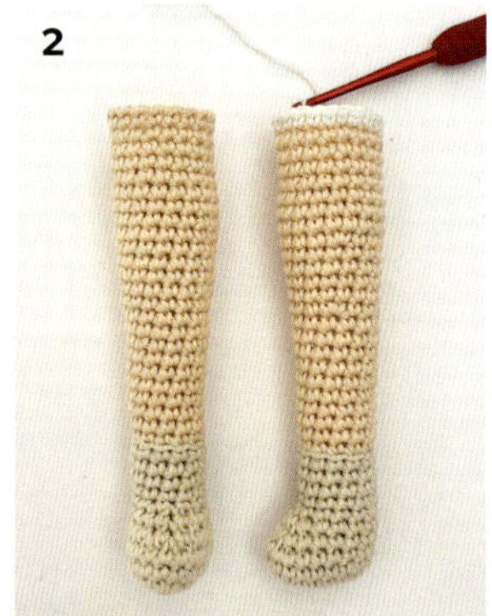

3

4

Body

Use yarns (R), (B), (I) and (A). Stuff as you go. Lay the two legs side by side, toes up and with second leg still on the hook: 2 ch and join to first leg with 1 dc (counts as first dc of round).

Round 1: 1 dc in each of 20 sts of first leg, 1 dc in 2 sts of chain, 1 dc in each of 20 sts of the other leg and 1 dc in 2 sts on other side of chain (20 + 2 + 20 + 2 = 44 sts) *(see photo 3)*. Place stitch marker here (it will be on doll's front).
Rounds 2–9: 1 dc in each st around (44 sts).
Round 10: work 32 dc (32 sts), changing to yarn (B) on last yrh.
Move stitch marker.

Round 11: 1 dc in each st around (44 sts).
Round 12: (dc2tog, 20 dc) twice (42 sts), changing to yarn (I) on last yrh to make the body (cut yarns (R) and (B) and weave in ends).
Round 13: 1 dc in blo of each st around (42 sts).
Round 14: (5 dc, dc2tog) six times (36 sts).
Rounds 15–22: 1 dc in each st around (36 sts).
Round 23: (4 dc, dc2tog) six times (30 sts).
Round 24: 1 dc in each st around (30 sts).
Round 25: (3 dc, dc2tog) six times (24 sts).
Round 26: 1 dc in each st around (24 sts).
Round 27: (4 dc, dc2tog) four times (20 sts).
Round 28: (3 dc, dc2tog) four times (16 sts), changing to yarn (A) on last yrh.
Round 29: 1 dc in blo of each st around (16 sts).
Cut yarn (I) and weave in end.
Round 30: (6 dc, dc2tog) twice (14 sts).

Note: this is the start of the 'tube' on to which the head will be fixed.

Rounds 31–36: 1 dc in each st around (14 sts).
Round 37: (5 dc, dc2tog) twice (12 sts).
Rounds 38–41: 1 dc in each st around (12 sts).
Finish stuffing.
Round 42: 6 dc2tog (6 sts).
Sew up the opening with a darning needle, leaving around 30cm (12in) of yarn to sew the head on at a later stage *(see photo 4)*.

***Note: to make the neck more stable, slip a pipe cleaner (chenille stick) into the opening** (see photo 5 of the mother's head, page 33).*

Embroider a line along round 10 in backstitch, using blue embroidery thread, to highlight the waist of the underpants.

5

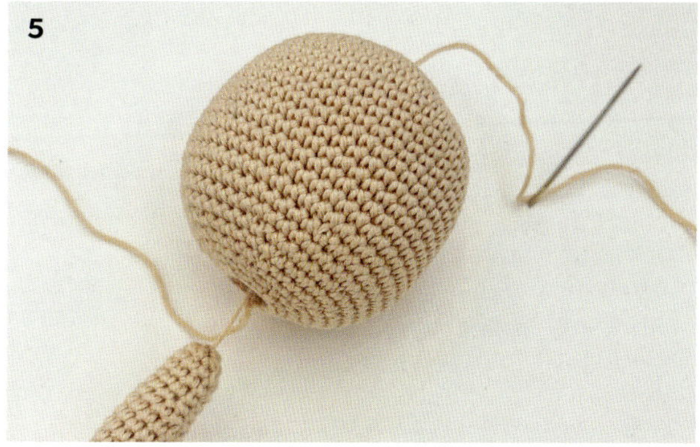

Head

Use yarn (A).
Round 1: 6 dc into a MR (6 sts).
Round 2: 2 dc in each st around (12 sts).
Round 3: (1 dc, 2 dc in the next st) six times (18 sts).
Round 4: (2 dc, 2 dc in the next st) six times (24 sts).
Round 5: (3 dc, 2 dc in the next st) six times (30 sts).
Round 6: (4 dc, 2 dc in the next st) six times (36 sts).
Round 7: (5 dc, 2 dc in the next st) six times (42 sts).
Round 8: (6 dc, 2 dc in the next st) six times (48 sts).
Round 9: (11 dc, 2 dc in the next st) four times (52 sts).
Rounds 10–20: 1 dc in each st around (52 sts).
Round 21: (11 dc, dc2tog) four times (48 sts).
Round 22: 1 dc in each st around (48 sts).
Round 23: 3 dc, dc2tog, (6 dc, dc2tog) five times, 3 dc (42 sts).
Start stuffing and continue as you go.
Round 24: (5 dc, dc2tog) six times (36 sts).
Round 25: 2 dc, dc2tog, (4 dc, dc2tog) five times, 2 dc (30 sts).
Round 26: (3 dc, dc2tog) six times (24 sts).
Round 27: 1 dc, dc2tog, (2 dc, dc2tog) five times, 1 dc (18 sts).
Round 28: (2 dc, dc2tog) four times, 2 dc (14 sts).
Join the round with 1 sl st and leave a long tail of yarn for sewing up.
Finish stuffing.
Prepare the opening into which the 'tube' will be inserted, using the handle of the crochet hook to help.
Thread a long needle with the tail of yarn from the 'tube' and pass it up through the opening in the head, bringing it out on top. Use this yarn to guide the head on to the tube until it reaches round 31. This will make it more stable. Knot yarn at top of head and weave in ends *(see photo 5)*.
Sew the head to the neck, passing the darning needle through the loops of the sts of the last round of the head and between the sts of the neck. Cut yarn and weave in end.

Project continues overleaf

Arm (make two)

Use yarns (A) and (I).

Start with yarn (A).

Round 1: 6 dc into a MR (6 sts).
Round 2: 2 dc in each st around (12 sts).
Rounds 3–5: 1 dc in each st around (12 sts).
Round 6: 5 dc, 1 bobble st (thumb), 6 dc (12 sts).
Round 7: 1 dc in each st around (12 sts).
Round 8: 2 dc, dc2tog, 5 dc, dc2tog, 1 dc (10 sts).
Rounds 9 and 10: 1 dc in each st around (10 sts).
Stuff hand lightly (using a wooden skewer or crochet hook handle to help).

Continue with yarn (I).

Rounds 11–20: 1 dc in each st around (10 sts).
Round 21: (4 dc, 2 dc in the next st) twice (12 sts).
Rounds 22–27: 1 dc in each st around (12 sts).
Pinch top of arm together, ensuring that the thumb points to the side of the body (add or sk 1 dc if necessary) and sew up with 5 dc into sts on both sides at same time. Cut, leaving sufficient yarn for making up.

Sew the arms on either side of the body, at round 27, ensuring the thumbs are facing in the right direction *(see photo 6)*.

6

Moustache

Use Hobbii Diablo yarn (II) (work with it doubled for more thickness) – 3.5mm (UK 9, US E4) crochet hook.

***Note: it is also possible to make it using cotton yarn** (see page 17).*

(See 'Moustache' chart, right.)

Row 1: work 8 ch, then starting in second ch from hook, 1 dc, 1 tr, 1 htr, 1 sl st, 1 htr, 1 tr, 1 dc (7 sts). Leave a length of yarn so you can sew the moustache on at round 21 in the centre of the face.
Add a stitch to pinch the central sl st. Fasten off and weave in end *(see photo 7)*.

Moustache

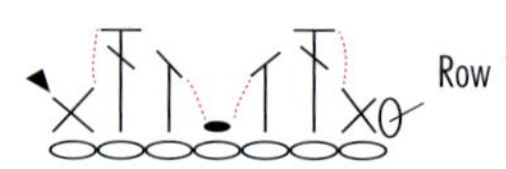

◄ Cut yarn.
○ **Chain stitch:** yrh, draw yarn through loop on the hook.
• **Slip stitch:** insert hook through first st, yrh and draw through st and loop on hook.
× **Double crochet:** insert hook through first st, yrh and draw through st, yrh and draw through both loops on hook.
T **1 half-treble:** yrh, insert hook through first st, yrh and draw through st, yrh and draw through all loops on hook.
Ŧ **1 treble:** yrh, insert hook through first st, yrh and draw through st then (yrh, draw through two loops) twice.

Hair

Use Hobbii Diablo yarn (II) (work with it doubled for more thickness) – 3.5mm (UK 9, US E4) crochet hook.

Note: it is also possible to use cotton yarn (see page 17).

Worked in rows.

Note: the 1 ch at the end of the row does not count as a stitch; it is only used to turn the work.

Row 1: work 36 ch, then starting in third ch from hook, 3 htr, 28 tr, 3 htr, 1 ch, turn (34 sts).
Row 2: 1 dc, 3 htr, 26 tr, 3 htr, 1 dc, 1 ch, turn (34 sts).
Row 3: 1 dc, 3 htr, 26 tr, 3 htr, 1 dc (34 sts).
Leave a long tail of yarn for sewing up. Sew on hair between rounds 13 and 14 of head, leaving a space of 18 sts at the front (insert pins as markers) *(see photos 8 and 9)*.

Cut yarn and weave in ends.

7

Tip
Gently brush the hair and moustache with a little metal brush to make the fibres stand out.

Using dark brown (or black) embroidery thread, embroider the eyes at round 19 (tenth round from the bottom of the head), spacing them 10 sts apart.

The trousers

Use yarns (S), (F) and (AA).

Use yarn (S).

Round 1: work 46 ch, then join with 1 dc into first ch (counts as first st of round), ensuring that the chain is not twisted) and work 1 dc in each st around (46 sts).
Rounds 2–4: 1 dc in each st around (46 sts).
Round 5: 12 dc, 2 dc in the next sts, 20 dc, 2 dc in the next st, 12 dc (48 sts).
Rounds 6–11: 1 dc in each st around (48 sts).
Mark the mid-point between the legs. Allow 23 sts for each leg.

Note: 1 dc remains free on either side of mid-point (mark with pins).

Join the last st of the back to the first st of the front with 1 dc (counts as first dc of round).

The sts of first leg now form a round *(see photo 10)*. Continue working as follows:

Rounds 12–34: 1 dc in each st around (23 sts); work 3 or 4 dc to arrive at mid-point between the legs.
Round 35: 1 sl st in blo of each st around (23 sts).
Cut yarn and weave in end.

Second leg: join yarn in back of work, next to pin and work 1 dc in each of next 23 sts (23 sts). Join in a round and repeat rounds 13 to 35 (23 sts).
Cut yarn and weave in ends.
Sew up opening between legs with a needle.
Weave in end.

Waistband

Use yarn (S).
Join the yarn in first st of round 1 and work 1 dc in each st around (46 sts).
Finish with 1 sl st. Cut yarn and weave in ends.

Embroider a line in backstitch just below the waistband using dark embroidery thread, to highlight the waist.

8

9

10

Project continues overleaf

Braces

Use yarn (F).

Note: worked in rows.

Row 1: work 33 ch, then starting in second ch from hook, 1 dc in next 8 ch (forms the back of the braces), then work 25 ch to form second strap.
Row 2: starting in second ch from hook, work 24 dc along this chain, then 24 dc along the first chain.
Cut yarn and weave in ends.

Fastening (make three)

Use yarn (AA).
Row 1: work 11 ch, then starting in second ch from hook, 1 dc, 8 sl st, 1 dc (10 sts). Fasten off to secure, leaving a long tail *(see photo 11)*.
Sew the fastenings at the end of each strap, pinching slightly in the centre and at the bottom of the back. Then sew the fastenings to the waistband of the trousers in the middle of the back and on the front, spaced 6 sts apart.
Weave in ends.
For buttons, work French knots using a contrasting thread at the end of each fastening *(see photo 12)*.

Note: it is also possible to sew on real buttons.

Embroider stripes in backstitch over the whole body and arms, alternating brown and navy blue embroidery thread, spaced 2 rows apart *(see photo 13)*. Ensure that the joins are centred on the back of the arms and body (under the braces) *(see photo 14)*.

The waistcoat

Using Merino Essentiel 3 yarn (EE).

Note: it is also possible to use cotton yarn.

Worked in rows.

Note: the 1 ch at the end of the row does not count as a stitch; it is only used to turn the work.

Row 1: work 21 ch, then starting in the second ch from hook, 1 dc in each st across, 1 ch, turn (20 sts).
Row 2: 2 dc in the next st, 7 ch, sk 6 sts, 6 dc, 7 ch, sk 6 sts, 2 dc in the next st, 1 ch, turn (24 sts).
Row 3: 1 dc in each st across, 1 ch, turn (24 sts).
Row 4: 2 dc in the next st, 6 dc, 2 dc in the next st, 8 dc, 2 dc in the next st, 6 dc, 2 dc in the next st, 1 ch, turn (28 sts).
Row 5: 1 dc in each st across, 1 ch, turn (28 sts).
Row 6: (2 dc in the next st, 8 dc) three times, 2 dc in the next st, 1 ch, turn (32 sts).

11

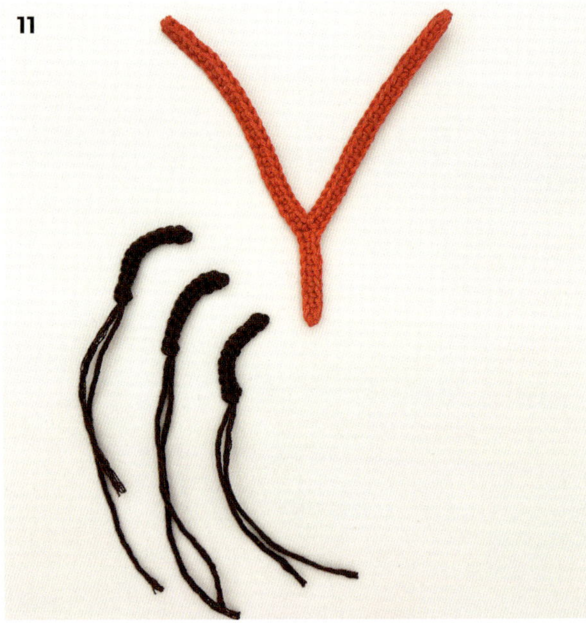

12

13

Row 7: 2 dc in the next st, 8 dc, 2 dc in the next st, 12 dc, 2 dc in the next st, 8 dc, 2 dc in the next st, 1 ch, turn (36 sts).
Rows 8–11: 1 dc in each st across, 1 ch, turn (36 sts).
Row 12: 10 dc, 2 dc in the next st, 14 dc, 2 dc in the next st, 10 dc, 1 ch, turn (38 sts).
Rows 13–16: 1 dc in each st across, 1 ch, turn (38 sts).
Row 17: (12 dc, 2 dc in the next st) twice, 12 dc, 1 ch, turn (40 sts).
Rows 18–22: 1 dc in each st across, 1 ch, turn (40 sts).
Do not cut yarn but crochet a border of 22 htr on the front of the waistcoat (working in the spaces between the rows), 1 ch, 20 dc around the neckhole, 1 ch, 22 htr on the other side (once again working in the spaces between the rows), 1 ch, then 40 htr round the bottom of the waistcoat.
Finish with 1 sl st into ch.
Cut yarn and weave in ends invisibly *(see photo 15)*.

If necessary, mist the waistcoat with water and iron to flatten out.

Shoe (make two)

Use yarns (AA) and (E).
Start with the sole using yarn (AA).
Work 8 ch.

Note: sts will be crocheted on both sides of chain.

Round 1: starting in second ch from hook, 6 dc, 3 dc in first ch; continue on other side. 5 dc, 2 dc in the next st (16 sts).
Round 2: 2 dc in the next st, 5 dc, 2 dc in next 3 sts, 6 dc, 2 dc in the next st (21 sts).
Round 3: 2 dc in the next st, 8 dc, 2 dc in next 3 sts, 8 dc, 2 dc in the next st (26 sts).
Round 4: 1 dc in blo of each st around (26 sts), changing to yarn (E) on last yrh.
Rounds 5 and 6: 1 dc in each st around (26 sts).
Round 7: 9 dc, 4 dc2tog, 9 dc (22 sts).
Round 8: 9 dc, 2 dc2tog, 9 dc (20 sts).
Round 9: 8 dc, 2 dc2tog, 8 dc (18 sts).
Round 10: 1 dc in each st around (18 sts).
Finish with 1 sl st, cut yarn and weave in ends.

Embroider three little lines using yarn (AA) on the front of the shoe for the laces *(see photo 16)*.

14

15

16

Project continues overleaf

Making the accessories (see photo 17)

17

Beret

Use yarn (BB).

Round 1: 6 dc into a MR (6 sts).
Round 2: 2 dc in each st around (12 sts).
Round 3: (1 dc, 2 dc in the next st) six times (18 sts).
Round 4: (2 dc, 2 dc in the next st) six times (24 sts).
Round 5: (3 dc, 2 dc in the next st) six times (30 sts).
Round 6: (4 dc, 2 dc in the next st) six times (36 sts).
Round 7: (5 dc, 2 dc in the next st) six times (42 sts).
Round 8: (6 dc, 2 dc in the next st) six times (48 sts).
Round 9: (7 dc, 2 dc in the next st) six times (54 sts).
Round 10: (8 dc, 2 dc in the next st) six times (60 sts).
Round 11: (9 dc, 2 dc in the next st) six times (66 sts).
Round 12: (10 dc, 2 dc in the next st) six times (72 sts).
Rounds 13–18: 1 dc in each st around (72 sts).
Round 19: (10 dc, dc2tog) six times (66 sts).
Round 20: (9 dc, dc2tog) six times (60 sts).
Round 21: 1 sl st in each st around (60 sts).
Cut yarn and weave in ends.

Work 4 ch to make the little stalk on the beret, then starting in the second ch from hook, work 1 sl st in each st across (3 sts). Leave a length of yarn, then sew the stalk to the top of the beret at round 1.
Weave in ends *(see photo 18)*.

18

Boules

Use yarns (W) and (X) and a small bead.

Ball (make three)

Use yarn (W).

Round 1: 6 dc into a MR (6 sts).
Round 2: 2 dc in each st around (12 sts).
Round 3: (1 dc, 2 dc in the next st) six times (18 sts).
Rounds 4–7: 1 dc in each st around (18 sts).
Round 8: (1 dc, dc2tog) six times (12 sts).
Round 9: 6 dc2tog (6 sts).
Stuff.
Cut the yarn and draw the opening closed, passing the yarn through flo of the sts of round 9.
Weave in ends and cut remaining yarn.

Note: use the little bead as the jack (see photo 17).

19

Case

Use yarn (X).

Work 15 ch.

Note: sts will be crocheted on both sides of chain.

Round 1: starting in second ch from hook, 2 dc in the next st, 12 dc, 4 dc in first ch; continue on other side. 12 dc, 2 dc in the next st (32 sts).
Round 2: 2 dc in the next 2 sts, 12 dc, 2 dc in the next 4 sts, 12 dc, 2 dc in the next 2 sts (40 sts).
Round 3: 2 dc in the next 3 sts, 15 dc, 2 dc in next 4 sts, 17 dc, 2 dc in the next st (48 sts).
Round 4: 1 dc in blo of each st around (48 sts).
Rounds 5 and 6: 1 dc in each st around (48 sts).
Do not cut yarn but make the central strap as follows:

Work 23 ch. Join with 1 sl st in the twenty- fifth stitch of round 6, then work 22 sl st along the chain. Secure with 1 sl st in the next st. Do not cut the yarn, but continue with 8 sl st along round 6 (slip the 3 balls inside the case before continuing); 10 ch to form the first side strap and secure with 1 sl st in the edge facing it. Continue with 9 sl st along round 6 to return to the starting point *(see photo 19)*.

Cut yarn and weave in ends.

Join yarn (X) on the opposite end, at the point where the central strap is joined, work 8 sl st along round 6, then 10 ch to form the second side strap and secure with 1 sl st on the opposite edge (there is a gap of 5 sts between the two straps). Continue with 9 sl st along round 6 to return to the starting point.

Cut yarn and weave in end.

Handle

Row 1: work 9 ch, then starting in second ch from hook, 8 sl sts (8 sts).

Cut yarn, leaving enough to sew the handle to the top of the case.

Weave in ends *(see photo 20)*.

Gift

Use yarns (G) and (F).

The gift is worked in two parts: the box and the lid.

Box

Use yarn (G).

Round 1: 4 dc into a MR (4 sts).
Round 2: 2 dc in each st around (8 sts).
Round 3: (1 dc, 3 dc in next st) four times (16 sts).

Note: there will be one group of 3 dc at each corner.

Round 4: 2 dc, 3 dc in next st, (3 dc, 3 dc in next st) three times, 1 dc (24 sts).
Round 5: 3 dc, 3 dc in next st, (5 dc, 3 dc in next st) three times, 2 dc (32 sts).
Round 6: 4 dc, 3 dc in next st, (7 dc, 3 dc in next st) three times, 3 dc (40 sts).

20

21

Round 7: 1 dc in blo of each st around (40 sts).
Rounds 8–13: 1 dc in each st around (40 sts).
Finish with 1 sl st.

Cut yarn and weave in ends.

Slip a piece of cardboard into the bottom of the box and round the sides to make it more stable *(see photo 21)*.

Lid

Use yarn (G).

Rounds 1–6: follow rounds 1–6 of the box instructions.
Round 7: 6 dc, 2 dc in next st, (9 dc, 2 dc in next st) three times, 3 dc (44 sts).
Round 8: 1 dc in blo of each st around (44 sts).
Round 9: 1 dc in each st around (44 sts).
Finish the work with 1 sl st, leaving a long tail of yarn for sewing up.

Slip a piece of cardboard into the bottom of the lid to make it more stable, then put the lid on the box and sew into place with a few sts.

Ribbon

Use yarn (F).

Row 1: work 9 ch, then starting in second ch from hook, 1 dc, 1 htr, 1 tr, 1 dtr, 1 tr, 1 htr, 1 dc, 1 sl st to make the first loop of the bow, then 56 ch.

Then 1 dc, 1 htr, 1 tr, 1 dtr, 1 tr, 1 htr, 1 dc, 1 sl st to form the second loop of the bow.

Cut yarn and weave in ends.

Tie it or sew it round the present *(see photo 17)*.

Newspaper

Cut a few pieces from a newspaper measuring approximately 11 x 7cm (4¼ x 2¾in). Place on top of each other and fold into four. Hold in place with a small strip of sticky tape *(see photo 17)*.

Lucie

THE GRANDMA

Finished height: 27cm (10½in)

You will need

DMC Natura Just Cotton (4-ply/fingering) yarn, 50g/1¾oz/155m/170yd, in (P), (V), (A) and (H) and a little of yarns (R), (W), (F), (AA), (D), (I), (E), (U), (L) and (M)
Hobbii Diablo (1–3-ply/lace weight) yarn, 50g/1¾oz/225m/246yd, in (JJ), for the shrug and yarn (II), for the hair (it is also possible to use DMC Natura Just Cotton – see page 17)

Dark brown, black and pink embroidery thread
2.25mm (UK 13, US B1) crochet hook, 3mm (UK 11, US 2/3) crochet hook for the hair and the shawl
A small piece of paper
Three wooden beads, 1.5cm (½in), in diameter
A wooden skewer and two small beads
Small button
Basic tools and materials (see pages 10–12)

Special stitches:
Bobble stitch (3 tr for thumbs), front-post treble

cott

Making the doll

Note: unless stated otherwise, always work in spiral rounds using a 2.25mm (UK 13, US B1) crochet hook.

Body

Note: start with the legs.

Leg (make two)

Use yarn (P).

Stuff legs as you go.

Round 1: 6 dc into a MR (6 sts).
Round 2: 2 dc in each st around (12 sts).
Round 3: 1 dc in each st around (12 sts).
Rounds 4 and 5: 2 dc in the next st, 5 dc, dc2tog, 4 dc (12 sts).
Round 6: 1 dc, 2 dc in the next st, 5 dc, dc2tog, 3 dc (12 sts).
Rounds 7 and 8: 2 dc, 2 dc in the next st, 4 dc, dc2tog, 3 dc (12 sts).
Rounds 9 and 10: 2 dc, dc2tog, 4 dc, 2 dc in the next st, 3 dc (12 sts).
Rounds 11–14: 1 dc in each st around (12 sts).
Round 15: (3 dc, 2 dc in the next st) three times (15 sts).
Rounds 16–18: 1 dc in each st around (15 sts).
Round 19: (4 dc, 2 dc in the next st) three times (18 sts).
Rounds 20–22: 1 dc in each st around (18 sts).
Round 23: (5 dc, 2 dc in the next st) three times (21 sts).
Rounds 24–34: 1 dc in each st around (21 sts); work an additional 5 dc to reach the side of the leg. Finish with 1 sl st.
Cut yarn and weave in ends. Finish stuffing.

Crochet second leg in same way as far as round 34. Work 4 or 5 additional dc to reach inside of leg *(see photo 1)*. Do not cut the yarn but continue as follows:

Body

Use yarns (P), (V) and (A).

Stuff body as you go. Lay the two legs side by side, toes up and with second leg still on the hook: 1 ch and join to first leg with 1 dc (counts as first dc of round).

Round 1: 1 dc in each of 21 sts of first leg, 1 dc in chain, 1 dc in each of 21 sts of the other leg and 1 dc on other side of chain (21 + 1 + 21 + 1 = 44 sts) *(see photo 2)*.
Place stitch marker here (it will be on doll's front).

Round 2: 21 dc, 2 dc in the next st (middle of back), 22 dc (45 sts).
Rounds 3–9: 1 dc in each st around (45 sts).
Round 10: work 35 dc (35 sts), changing to yarn (V) on last yrh.
Move stitch marker.

Round 11: (all in blo). dc2tog, 20 dc, dc2tog, 9 dc, dc2tog, 10 dc (42 sts).

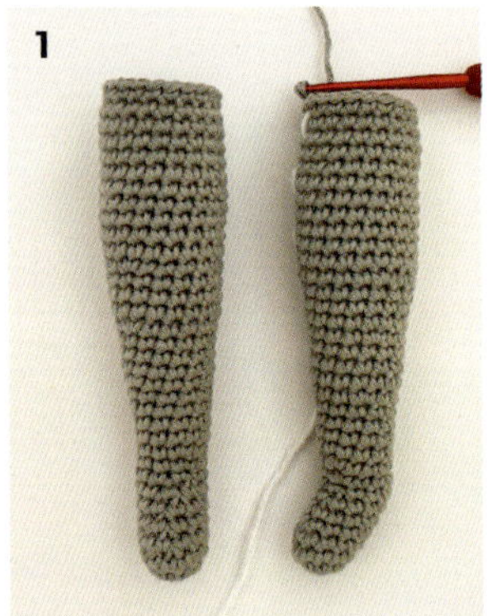
1

2

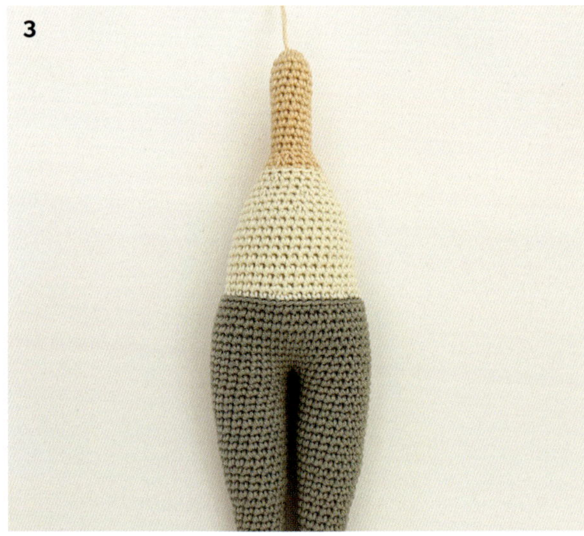
3

Round 12: (5 dc, dc2tog) six times (36 sts).
Rounds 13–20: 1 dc in each st around (36 sts).
Round 21: (4 dc, dc2tog) six times (30 sts).
Round 22: 1 dc in each st around (30 sts).
Round 23: (3 dc, dc2tog) six times (24 sts).
Round 24: 1 dc in each st around (24 sts).
Round 25: (4 dc, dc2tog) four times (20 sts), changing to yarn (A) on last yrh.
Round 26: 1 dc in blo of each st around (20 sts).
Round 27: (3 dc, dc2tog) four times (16 sts).
Round 28: (2 dc, dc2tog) four times (12 sts).

Note: this is the start of the 'tube' on to which the head will be fixed.

Rounds 29–40: 1 dc in each st around (12 sts).
Finish stuffing.

Round 41: 6 dc2tog (6 sts).
Sew up the opening with a darning needle, leaving 30cm (12in) of yarn to sew the head on at a later stage *(see photo 3)*.

Note: to make the neck more stable, slip a pipe cleaner (chenille stick) into the opening *(see photo 5, page 33).*

Head

Use yarn (A).

Round 1: 6 dc into a MR (6 sts).
Round 2: 2 dc in each st around (12 sts).
Round 3: (1 dc, 2 dc in the next st) six times (18 sts).
Round 4: (2 dc, 2 dc in the next st) six times (24 sts).
Round 5: (3 dc, 2 dc in the next st) six times (30 sts).
Round 6: (4 dc, 2 dc in the next st) six times (36 sts).
Round 7: (5 dc, 2 dc in the next st) six times (42 sts).
Round 8: (6 dc, 2 dc in the next st) six times (48 sts).
Round 9: (11 dc, 2 dc in the next st) four times (52 sts).
Rounds 10–20: 1 dc in each st around (52 sts).
Round 21: (11 dc, dc2tog) four times (48 sts).
Round 22: 1 dc in each st around (48 sts).
Round 23: 3 dc, dc2tog, (6 dc, dc2tog) five times, 3 dc (42 sts).

Start stuffing and continue as you go.

Round 24: (5 dc, dc2tog) six times (36 sts).
Round 25: 2 dc, dc2tog, (4 dc, dc2tog) five times, 2 dc (30 sts).
Round 26: (3 dc, dc2tog) six times (24 sts).
Round 27: 1 dc, dc2tog, (2 dc, dc2tog) five times, 1 dc (18 sts).
Round 28: (1 dc, dc2tog) six times (12 sts).

Join the round with 1 sl st and leave a long tail of yarn for sewing up.

Finish stuffing.

Prepare the opening into which the 'tube' will be inserted, using the handle of the crochet hook to help.

Thread a long needle with the tail of yarn from the 'tube' and pass it up through the opening in the head, bringing it out on top. Use this yarn to guide the head on to the tube until it reaches round 31. This will make it more stable. Knot yarn at top of head and weave in end *(see photos 8 to 10 of the mother's head on page 35)*.

Sew the head to the neck, passing the needle through the 2 loops of the sts of the last round of the head and between the sts of the neck.

Cut yarn and weave in ends *(see photo 4)*.

Arm (make two)

Crocheted separately using yarns (A) and (H).

Start with yarn (A).

Round 1: 5 dc into a MR (5 sts).
Round 2: 2 dc in each st around (10 sts).
Rounds 3–5: 1 dc in each st around (10 sts).
Round 6: 1 dc, 1 bobble st (thumb), 8 dc (10 sts).
Round 7: 1 dc in each st around (10 sts).
Round 8: 1 dc, dc2tog, 7 dc (9 sts).
Rounds 9 and 10: 1 dc in each st around (9 sts).

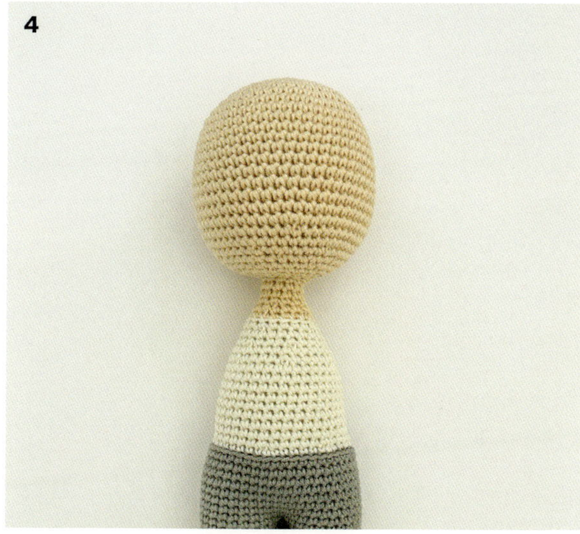

Stuff hand lightly, using a wooden skewer or crochet hook handle to help.

Continue with yarn (H).

Round 11: 1 dc in each st around (9 sts).
Round 12: 1 dc in blo of each st around (9 sts).
Rounds 13–17: 1 dc in each st around (9 sts).
Round 18: 8 dc, 2 dc in the next st (10 sts).
Rounds 19–26: 1 dc in each st around (10 sts).

Pinch top of arm together, ensuring that the thumb points to the side of the body (add or sk 1 dc if necessary) and sew up with 4 dc into sts on both sides at same time.

Cut, leaving sufficient yarn for making up.

Project continues overleaf

Sleeve turn-up

Use yarn (H).
Holding the hand upwards, join the yarn and work (1 dc, 1 ch) in each free loop of round 12.
Finish with 1 sl st in starting st, then cut yarn and weave in ends.

Sew the arms on either side of the body, at round 25 *(see photo 5)*, ensuring the thumbs are facing in the right direction.

Hair

Use Hobbii Diablo yarn (II) – 3mm (UK 11, US 2/3) crochet hook.

Note: it is also possible to use cotton yarn (see page 17).

Hairpiece

Round 1: 6 dc into a MR (6 sts).
Round 2: 2 dc in each st around (12 sts).
Round 3: (1 dc, 2 dc in the next st) six times (18 sts).
Round 4: (2 dc, 2 dc in the next st) six times (24 sts).
Round 5: (3 dc, 2 dc in the next st) six times (30 sts).
Round 6: (4 dc, 2 dc in the next st) six times (36 sts).
Round 7: (5 dc, 2 dc in the next st) six times (42 sts).
Round 8: (6 dc, 2 dc in the next st) six times (48 sts).
Round 9: (11 dc, 2 dc in the next st) four times (52 sts).
Rounds 10–22: 1 dc in each st around (52 sts). (The number of rounds can be adapted depending on the yarn used and your own crocheting style. Try the hairpiece before you work the last round.)
Do not fasten off but continue with the strands.
Round 23: 1 sl st, then rep (26 ch, starting in third chain from hook, 1 htr in each st across, sk 1 st on hairpiece and secure with 1 sl st in the next st) four times.
Leave a long tail of yarn for sewing up.

Bun (make two)

Round 1: 6 dc into a MR (6 sts).
Round 2: 2 dc in each st around (12 sts).
Round 3: (1 dc, 2 dc in the next st) six times (18 sts).
Rounds 4–6: 1 dc in each st around (18 sts).
Round 7: (1 dc, dc2tog) six times (12 sts).
Join the round with 1 sl st and leave a long tail of yarn for sewing up. Stuff lightly *(see photo 6)*.

Adjust the hairpiece on the head, positioning the long strands at the front. Hold in place with pins. Sew on the hairpiece, following the sts of the last round.
Cut yarn and weave in ends.
Sew the buns on either side of the head, over the join between the hair and the skin and sew two strands on either side with a few stitches *(see photo 7)*.
Knot or embroider a few strands on the forehead.

6

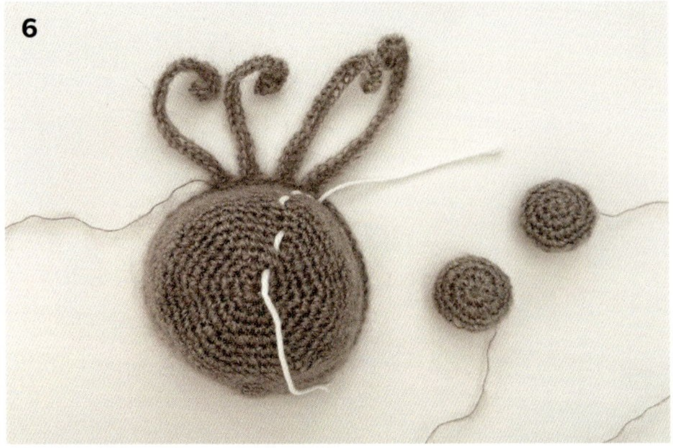

7

8

> *Tip*
> *Gently brush the hair with a little metal brush to make the fibres stand out.*

Using dark brown (or black) embroidery thread, embroider the eyes at round 19 (tenth round from the bottom of the head), spacing them 9 sts apart *(see photo 8)*.
For a healthy glow, add a little colour to her cheeks using a piece of cloth rubbed with a red crayon *(see photo 8)*.

Spectacles

Use yarn (D).
Use wire to make the spectacles, winding cotton yarn around to cover the wire (see instructions on page 16).

Dress

Use yarns (V) and (H).
Worked in rows.

Note: the 1 ch at the end of the row does not count as a stitch; it is only used to turn the work.

Start with yarn (V).
Row 1: work 25 ch, starting in second ch from hook, 1 dc in each st across, changing to yarn (H) in last yrh; 1 ch, turn (24 sts).
Row 2: (4 dc, 2 dc in the next st) twice, 4 dc, (2 dc in the next st, 4 dc) twice, 1 ch, turn (28 sts).

Row 3: 4 dc, 6 ch, sk 5 sts, 2 dc in the next st, 8 dc, 2 dc in the next st, 6 ch, sk 5 sts, 4 dc. 1 ch, turn (32 sts).
Row 4: 3 dc, 2 dc in the next st, 6 dc, 2 dc in the next st, 10 dc, 2 dc in the next st, 6 dc, 2 dc in the next st, 3 dc, 1 ch, turn (36 sts).
Rows 5–8: 1 dc in each st across, 1 ch, turn (36 sts).
Row 9: (5 dc, 2 dc in the next st) twice, 12 dc, (2 dc in the next st, 5 dc) twice, 1 ch, turn (40 sts).
Row 10: 1 dc in each st across, 1 ch, turn (40 sts).
Row 11: 14 dc, 2 dc in the next st, 10 dc, 2 dc in the next st, 14 dc, 1 ch, turn (42 sts).
Row 12: 1 dc in each st across, 1 ch, turn (42 sts).
Row 13: 8 dc, 2 dc in the next st, 24 dc, 2 dc in the next st, 8 dc, 1 ch, turn (44 sts); 1 ch, turn.
Row 14: 1 dc in each st across, 1 ch, turn (44 sts).
Row 15: (14 dc, 2 dc in the next st) twice, 14 dc, 1 ch, turn (46 sts).
Row 16: 1 dc in each st across, 1 ch, turn (46 sts).
Row 17: 8 dc, 2 dc in the next st, 28 dc, 2 dc in the next st, 8 dc, 1 ch, turn (48 sts).
Rows 18–21: 1 dc in each st across, 1 ch, turn (48 sts).
Row 22: (8 dc, 2 dc in the next st) twice, 12 dc, (2 dc in the next st, 8 dc) twice, 1 ch, turn (52 sts).
Rows 23–32: 1 dc in each st across, 1 ch, turn (52 sts).
Row 33: 1 dc in each st around (52 sts).
Fasten off, leaving a long tail of yarn for making up *(see photo 9)*.

Decorative edge round bottom of the dress

Use yarn (V).
Join yarn in blo of last st of row 33, then crochet (1 dc, 3 ch) in each st across.
Fasten off, leaving a 40cm (16in) length of yarn to embroider a line in backstitch along flo of sts of row 33. Weave in ends.
Sew up opening on back from bottom over approximately 20 rounds using waiting yarn (H), then weave in all ends. Join two short pieces of yarn to the top corners of the back so it can be tied on.

Note: it is also possible to sew on a button and make a button loop.

Shrug

Use Hobbii Diablo yarn (JJ) – 3mm (UK 11, US 2/3) crochet hook *(see photo 10)*.

Note: it is also possible to use cotton yarn; this has been used in the step-by-step photograph so the stitches can be seen more easily.

Worked in rows.

Note: the 1 ch at the end of the row does not count as a stitch; it is only used to turn the work.

Row 1: work 32 ch, then starting in second ch from hook, work 1 dc in each st across, 1 ch, turn (31 sts).
Row 2: sk 2 sts, 1 sl st, 1 dc, 2 htr, 10 tr, 3 tr in the next st, 10 tr, 2 htr, 1 dc, 1 sl st, 1 ch, turn (31 sts).

9

10

11

12

Row 3: sk 2 sts, 1 sl st, 1 dc, 2 htr, 9 tr, 3 tr in the next st, 9 tr, 2 htr, 1 dc, 1 ch, sk 2 sts, 1 sl st, 1 ch, turn (30 sts).
Row 4: sk 2 sts, 1 sl st, 1 dc, 2 htr, 9 tr, 3 tr in the next st, 9 tr, 2 htr, 1 dc, 1 ch, sk 1 st, 1 sl st (30 sts); 1 sl st in each of next 2 sts to reach end of row in order to work frills along row 4 *(see photo 11)*.
Row 5: (decorative border). 3 ch, turn then (1 sl st, 3 ch) in each st to penultimate st, (1 sl st, 5 ch) in the penultimate st to form a buttonhole.
Secure with 1 sl st in the last st.
Cut yarn and weave in ends.
Sew a little button on to the opposite corner *(see photo 12)*.

Project continues overleaf

Ballet pump (make two)

Use yarn (AA) *(see photo 13)*.
Work 8 ch.

Note: sts will be crocheted on both sides of chain.

Round 1: starting in second ch from hook, 2 dc in next st, 5 dc, 4 dc in first ch; continue on other side. 5 dc, 2 dc in next st (18 sts).
Round 2: 2 dc in the next st, 6 dc, 2 dc in each of next 4 sts, 6 dc, 2 dc in the next st (24 sts).
Round 3: 1 dc in each st around (24 sts).
Round 4: 8 dc, 8 htr, 8 dc (24 sts).
Round 5: 9 dc, 8 htr, 7 dc (24 sts).
Round 6: 9 dc, 4 dc2tog, 7 dc (20 sts).
Round 7: 8 sl st, 5 ch, sk 6 sts, 6 sl st (19 sts).
Cut yarn and weave in ends.

13

Making the accessories *(see photo 14)*

Basket

Use yarns (E), (F), (I) and (U).
Start with yarn (E).
Round 1: 6 dc into a MR (6 sts).
Round 2: 2 dc in each st around (12 sts).
Round 3: (1 dc, 2 dc in the next st) six times (18 sts).
Round 4: (2 dc, 2 dc in the next st) six times (24 sts).
Round 5: (3 dc, 2 dc in the next st) six times (30 sts).
Round 6: (4 dc, 2 dc in the next st) six times (36 sts).
Round 7: (5 dc, 2 dc in the next st) six times (42 sts).
Round 8: 1 dc in blo of each st around (42 sts), changing to yarn (F) on last yrh.
Round 9: (to form the wicker effect) (1 dc, 1 dc in st of round 7) twenty-one times (42 sts), changing to yarn (E) on last yrh.
Round 10: (1 dc in st of round 8, 1 dc) twenty-one times (42 sts), changing to yarn (I) on last yrh.
Round 11: (1 dc, 1 dc in st of round 9) twenty-one times (42 sts).
Continue, using yarn (E).
Round 12: (1 dc in st of round 10, 1 dc) twenty-one times (42 sts), changing to yarn (U) on last yrh.
Round 13: (1 dc, 1 dc in st of round 11) twenty-one times (42 sts).
Continue, using yarn (E).
Round 14: (1 dc in st of round 12, 1 dc) twenty-one times (42 sts).
Continue, using yarn (F).
Round 15: (1 dc, 1 dc in st of round 13) twenty-one times (42 sts).
Continue using yarn (E).
Round 16: (1 dc in st of round 14, 1 dc) twenty-one times (42 sts).
Round 17: 1 sl st in each st around (42 sts).

14

15

Round 18: crochet the handle, work 22 ch, sk 20 sts, 1 sl st in the next st, passing the hook from the inside to the outside, then 22 sl st along the chain.
Cut yarn and weave in ends *(see photo 15)*.

Balls of wool

In several colours of your choice *(see photo 16)*.

Large skeins of wool

Worked in joined rounds with front-post trebles.
Round 1: 2 ch (counts as first tr), 9 tr into a MR (10 sts); join round with 1 sl st in 2 ch.
Round 2: 2 ch (counts as first tr), 1 front-post tr, around the post of each tr of previous round (10 sts) *(see photo 17)*; join with 1 sl st in second of 2 ch.
Round 3: rep round 2.
Round 4: 1 ch, 1 dc in each st around (10 sts); join with 1 sl st.
Round 5: 2 ch (counts as first tr), 1 tr in each st of previous round (10 sts); join with 1 sl st in 2 ch.
Round 6: 2 ch (counts as first tr), 1 front-post tr, round the post of each tr of previous round (10 sts); join with 1 sl st in second of 2 ch.
Fasten off, leaving enough yarn for making up.
Stuff ball lightly and sew up the opening with the darning needle, passing the needle through flo of the sts. Pull tight and weave in end. You could also unroll it in the centre and allow a short length to hang out, or to stick a paper band around the ball *(see photo 18)*.

Small skeins of wool

Worked in spiral rounds, using simple trebles.
Round 1: 2 ch (counts as first tr), 7 tr into a MR (8 sts).
Round 2: 1 dc in each st around (8 sts).
Round 3: 1 sl st, 2 ch (counts as first tr), 1 tr into each st around (8 sts).
Join the round with 1 sl st into second of 2 ch.
Fasten off, leaving enough yarn for making up.
Stuff ball gently and sew up the opening with the darning needle, passing the needle through flo of the sts.
Pull tight and weave in end.

Stick a paper band around the skein.

For the round balls, wrap the yarn around a wooden bead (1.5cm (¾in) in diameter) adding a dab of glue from time to time. Leave a short length of thread to hang.

Knitting needles

Using a wooden skewer and 2 small beads: cut the skewer so you have 2 lengths of 7cm (2¾in), apply a dab of glue to one end and insert into a bead. Shape the other end with a cutter if you wish.

16

17

18

Project continues overleaf

Cat

Use yarns (W) and (H) and a little black and pink embroidery thread to embroider the face *(see photo 19)*.

Head

Use yarn (W).

Stuff the head as you go.

Round 1: 6 dc into a MR (6 sts).
Round 2: 2 dc in each st around (12 sts).
Round 3: (1 dc, 2 dc in the next st) six times (18 sts).
Round 4: 1 dc in each st around (18 sts).
Round 5: (5 dc, 2 dc in the next st) three times (21 sts).
Rounds 6–8: 1 dc in each st around (21 sts).
Round 9: (1 dc, dc2tog) seven times (14 sts).
Round 10: 7 dc2tog (7 sts).

Cut a length of yarn and sew up the opening with the darning needle, passing the needle through flo of the sts of the last round to pull tight. Weave in end.

Body

Use yarn (W).

Stuff the body as you go.

Round 1: 6 dc into a MR (6 sts).
Round 2: 2 dc in each st around (12 sts).
Round 3: (1 dc, 2 dc in the next st) six times (18 sts).
Round 4: (2 dc, 2 dc in the next st) six times (24 sts).
Round 5: 10 dc, 1 bobble st (paw), 2 dc, 1 bobble st (paw), 10 dc (24 sts).
Rounds 6 and 7: 1 dc in each st around (24 sts).
Round 8: 3 dc2tog, 12 dc, 3 dc2tog (18 sts).
Round 9: dc2tog, 14 dc, dc2tog (16 sts).
Round 10: (2 dc, dc2tog) four times (12 sts).
Join round with 1 sl st.

Fasten off, leaving a length of yarn to sew the body under the head. At the chin, weave the yarn between the sts of the body rather than under the loops of the last round, to pull the head down slightly.

Fasten off and weave in ends.

Ear (make two)

Use yarn (W).

Work 4 ch, then starting in second ch from hook, 1 dc, 1 htr, 1 tr along the chain.

Fasten off, leaving a length of yarn to sew the ears to the head at rounds 3 and 4.

Weave in the starting yarn.

Tail

Use yarn (W).

Round 1: 4 dc into a MR (4 sts).
Rounds 2–9: 1 dc in each st around (4 sts). Join the round with 1 sl st, leaving a long tail of yarn to sew the tail to the bottom of the back.

Fasten off and weave in end *(see photo 20)*.

Embroider the eyes with the black embroidery thread at round 6, spaced 4 sts apart and the nose in pink in the middle.

19

20

Collar

Use yarn (H).

Work 14 ch, then tie around the neck.

Weave in ends.

Discover the whole world of Lulu Compotine
on Instagram @luciennecompotine

Share your creations on Instagram using the hashtags #luluscrochetdolls and #lulucompotine

First published in the UK in 2027 by
Search Press Limited
Wellwood, North Farm Road,
Tunbridge Wells, Kent TN2 3DR

1 2 3 4 5 6 7 8 9 10

Original title:
La famille de Lulu au crochet © Les éditions de saxe 2024

Creator: Lulu Compotine
Photography: Lulu Compotine
Illustrations: Céline Bonnaud
Page-setting: Christine Lim
Technical drawings: Céline Cantat

English translation from French by Burravoe Translation Services

ISBN: 978-1-80092-447-5
ebook ISBN: 978-1-80093-397-2

Bookmarked Hub
A bonus project can be found and downloaded free from the Bookmarked Hub. Search for this book by title or ISBN: the project can be found under 'Book Extras'. Membership of the Bookmarked online community is free: www.bookmarkedhub.com

Publishers' notes
Metric measurements are used in this book; the imperial conversions are rounded to the nearest ¼in. Always use either metric or imperial measurements, not a combination of both.

UK crochet terms are used throughout this book. For UK to US equivalents please refer to page 12 and the inside front cover.

The Publishers and author can accept no responsibility for any consequences arising from the information, advice or instructions given in this publication.

For errata, please visit our website (www.searchpress.com) or the Bookmarked Hub (www.bookmarkedhub.com).

GPSR information can be found at www.searchpress.com
Printed in China, TT062026.

MIX
Paper | Supporting responsible forestry
FSC® C016973
FSC www.fsc.org